First published in March 2015

A catalogue record for this book is available from the
British Library.

ISBN 978 0 85733 798 6

Library of Congress control no. 2014949121

Published by Haynes Publishing,
Sparkford, Yeovil,
Somerset BA22 7JJ, UK.
Tel: 01963 442030 Fax: 01963 440001
Int. tel: +44 1963 442030
Int. fax: +44 1963 440001
E-mail: sales@haynes.co.uk
Website: www.haynes.co.uk

Haynes North America Inc.,
861 Lawrence Drive, Newbury Park,
California 91320, USA.

Printed in the USA by Odcombe Press LP,
1299 Bridgestone Parkway, La Vergne,
TN 37086.

Cover images:
© Discovery Communications/James Cheadle
© Discovery Communications/Gary Moyes

WHEELER DEALERS

2003 onwards (10 car restoration projects)

Car Restoration Manual

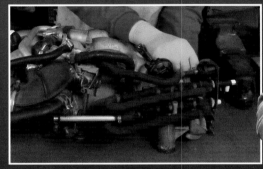

The most popular restorations from the **Discovery** CHANNEL™ TV series

Chris Randall, with Mike Brewer and Edd China

Contents

Forewords

People often say I have the luckiest job in the world, and as I read through the chapters in this book and look back at our adventures over the last 12 years and 101 cars I have to agree.

Wheeler Dealers started life as a small show that both Edd and I care passionately about. Some folk ask if we knew it would be this popular, and the truth is, yes. When you work as hard at something as us and the crew, and sacrifice a lot of your personal life, there has to be success. These days *Wheeler Dealers* is enjoyed by fans almost everywhere on the planet, and that audience keeps growing. We can only thank you, the fans who have stuck by us and the show, even when it may not have been the best car to do (Suzuki SJ410) or the best repair job (Ford Capri) – you still tuned in to enjoy our adventures.

I need to thank Attaboy TV for their dedication to the show since day one, especially Michael Wood and Daniel Allum. Thanks to our amazing film crew who give up so much of their lives so we can bring you the show, Nick Avery (DOP), John Sterling (DOP), Simon Edwards (sound), Dave Chapman (sound), and the many others we have had the pleasure of working with in the past. Thanks to Discovery and Velocity Channel for the chance to do this show and expand into new territories. Special thanks to Chris Randall, and his wonderful wife Rebecca, without whose tireless dedication and Beck's cups of tea this book would never have been written. Thanks too to my screen partner Edd China (and Imogen) for 12 years of fun and true friendship that never tires, and his dedication to the real stars of the show (the cars). But the biggest dedication of all goes to my soulmate, friend, business partner and beautiful wife Michelle, who has pushed this show and its success all the way, together with the support of our daughter Chloe. Girls, I love you. In fact, I love you all.

Thanks, and enjoy the book. It's cracking!

Mike Brewer
@mikebrewer

Top Tip; always be curious, even if you are crazy busy, and always try to say 'yes' to new experiences, just to see what comes of it. Also, every once in a while, just stop, have a look around and count your blessings!

Way back in the Spring of 2002 I was ridiculously busy working fourteen- and fifteen-hour days at Cummfy Banana, building a street-legal driving office while at the same time trying to create a giant drivable shopping trolley. Business was good, but deadlines were tight, Paul was giving me a hand as always, and even with the help of another eight or so people we were really up against it. My first foray into television, BBC2's Panic Mechanic, was also just on air, so on top of the work, more enquiries were coming in than usual. One call asked if I would like to audition for a new car show for Discovery. I was so busy I turned them down, but they gave me a date and an address, and said to pop in if I changed my mind. Curiosity got the better of me, and as it turned out I had to have a meeting just fifteen minutes away from the screen test, on the same date. I believe in things happening for a reason, so I thought 'why not'?...

...Some weeks later, having forgotten about the 'interview', I received another call, and this time the guys wanted to bring TV's Mike Brewer along to try us out together. We hit it off instantly, and the rest is history. None of us had a clue that the show would be so successful and in so many countries around the World. Demand for more episodes is so great I find myself writing this under the California sun, trying to beat the British winter by filming half of our next forty episodes from a place where the weather is a little more reliable.

So, as I take a rare break from our busy filming schedule to write this, I'm pondering how far we have come. 101 episodes, international notoriety (or at least infamy) and I get to play with classic cars all day. Lucky my curiosity got the better of me!

None of this would have happened if it wasn't for Mike Wood and Dan Allum, who came up with the idea for Grand Autos all those years ago – thanks guys for making that phone call.

Thanks also must go to Leone Hutchinson for commissioning the series in the first place, and Victoria Noble for taking it on to the next level.

Creating each episode is a huge undertaking, and takes many hours of blood, sweat and tears, so I would also like to thank the team who support us so we can share our passion with you and bring it to the screen; the ever present Paul Brackley and new boy 'Northern' Phil, our silent little mechanic helpers, and of course the wand-waving crew who make us look good enough to be on TV, John Sterling, Nick Avery, Simon 'Bear' Edwards, 'Diamond' Dave Chapman and Tas who keeps us all on track, and the rest of our extended dysfunctional telly family at Attaboy TV. We certainly couldn't do this without you all.

Thanks Mike for the years of fun and friendship, and the endless hours of hot air we have shared in cars waiting for the next shot, my team at Grease Junkie who crack on despite my constant absence, and of course my considerably better half Imogen who is my world – thank you for your enduring patience with everything I get up to.

Thanks to Chris for taking on this task, especially as pinning me down for interrogation was like herding kittens!

Finally, thanks to you for sharing our adventures for all of these years – we'll keep making them if you keep watching them!

Introduction

Wheeler Dealers. It's a show that's had car enthusiasts of all ages riveted since it first appeared way back in 2003, and it's since gone on to become a global phenomenon. In fact during the 12 months of 2014, the total worldwide viewing figures for all series broadcast reached 159 million!

The show follows the adventures of Mike Brewer and Edd China as they buy, restore and sell classic cars, and has almost certainly been responsible for inspiring enthusiasts across the globe to imitate their adventures. And if you love cars as much as they do – as much as we all do, in fact – then the sight of neglected cars being rescued from an appointment with the scrapyard, and being given a new lease of life, is surely a heart-warming one. Let's not forget too that *Wheeler Dealers* isn't just an entertainment show for television – Mike and Edd have been around cars for more years than they care to remember, and their enthusiasm and excitement when it comes to restoring classics comes through loud and clear.

Having spent so much time with them during the course of writing this book I can say without fear of contradiction that they care deeply about the job they are doing, and pour a huge amount of time and effort into making sure the finished project is as good as it can possibly be. This really is about aiming to keep important vehicles on the road so that they can be enjoyed by us car nuts for years to come.

For my own part I came to *Wheeler Dealers* quite late in its life, 2010 in fact, but I clearly remember the day when I discovered just how enjoyable – and indeed addictive – it is, and I only wish that I'd found it sooner. Still, I've certainly made up for that since, avidly watching every episode I can get my hands on, and, as my wife will attest, often watching them more than once. But that's what the show is like. I'm sure I speak for many of its fans when I say that it's something

you can never really tire of, that there is always something new to spot, and I know I've spent (far too many) hours daydreaming of rescuing and restoring my very own classic just like Mike and Edd. One day for sure.

It all started in 2003 with the restoration of a Porsche 924, and no one – least of all Mike and Edd – knew just how big the show would become. Its budget was tiny, with just £1,000 available to buy and restore the car, and while that might seem laughable now let's not forget that up until *Wheeler Dealers* came along no one had attempted to film the restoration of a car for a TV show, and it wasn't without its challenges. The presenters had to get used to working together, and filming wasn't straightforward either, as detailed mechanical and body repairs, tight production schedules and delicate camera equipment didn't seem a match made in heaven.

Thankfully for us they persevered, but it hasn't always been plain sailing across the years. Some of the projects didn't go quite as planned, putting pressure on budgets and leading to many late nights in the workshop, and there have been the odd disagreements too. Who can forget Mike's dismay at being confronted with a vivid yellow Ford Escort, for example, while Edd hasn't always been entirely happy with the amount of midnight oil that was sure to need burning when an especially decrepit car arrived at the workshop. It's no surprise really, given how much both presenters care about doing the job properly, but the partnership has endured for more than a decade and is undoubtedly one of the strongest and most entertaining on television today.

But over the past 12 years and more than 100 episodes the show has featured some amazing cars, from those that are familiar to just about every car enthusiast to some that are more than a little unusual and unique. From sports cars to luxury cruisers, from off-roaders to cars that float, and from the most vintage to the truly modern classic, there has been something for everyone. And surely I can't be the only person that would have been stumped if asked to describe an FSM Syrena before seeing it on the show?

So why feature the particular cars in this book? Well, for one thing I think that they represent the true core of what *Wheeler Dealers* has been about over the years, from its earliest days and tiny budgets to the exciting supercars that many of us

aspire to own. In between are classics that really fire the imagination, from true automotive legends like the Peugeot 205GTI and Jaguar E-Type that perfectly capture the flavour of their respective motoring decades, to something a little more quirky and unusual. Restoring a Second World War Jeep or an Amphicar isn't going to be something many of us will ever have the chance to do, but it's wonderful to see it being done by experts all the same.

I also wanted the book to reflect the huge range of restoration jobs that Mike and Edd have tackled over the years, from those that can be done on our driveways with a simple toolkit to the somewhat more ambitious that take skill and plenty of practice and experience. For me, it's not just the chance to see wonderful classic cars being enjoyed but the excitement of never knowing what they'll be doing next and learning new things that keeps me eagerly awaiting every new series and episode. And luckily for all of us avid fans, there are plenty more to come over the next few years, with another 40 cars all set to get the *Wheeler Dealers* treatment.

I hope you enjoy looking back over some fantastic projects, and perhaps you'll be inspired to have a go yourself. I know I am.

Chris Randall

Acknowledgements

Without Mike Brewer, Edd China and everyone behind the scenes there would be no show to write about. So huge thanks guys, as a car enthusiast I've loved every minute. Thanks should also go to all of the specialists and experts that have helped in making every show so enjoyable. When it came to writing this book I'd like to thank Mike for trusting that I could pull it off, Steve Rendle at Haynes Publishing for his help and patience, and Alison Paye and Darren Hollands at Discovery for their invaluable help in sourcing the pictures. And of course my wife Rebecca deserves special thanks for listening to me talk about *Wheeler Dealers* non-stop for so many months, and for being so patient when I wanted to watch an episode 'just one more time'. I couldn't have done it without her.

Austin Mini

◄ The Mini was sold in both Austin and Morris forms. This is the Morris Mini-Minor version and it shows the excellent standard the boys were aiming for.

The Austin Mini arrived in 1959, and thanks to the brilliance of Alec Issigonis it was a marvel of packaging and clever engineering, and pretty much set the template for all small cars since. Placing a wheel at each corner meant seating for four despite the tiny exterior dimensions – not to mention contributing to the great handling that would see Minis dominate rallying in the 1960s – while the transverse engine with the gearbox mounted beneath freed up yet more space. Sales weren't great to begin with and it would take until the mid-1960s before they really took off, but over a period of 41 years 5.5 million examples were made before the Rover Group finally pulled the plug on production in October 2000.

It was simply a terrific little car, but more importantly for programme viewers it was also one of the first to receive the *Wheeler Dealers* treatment way back in 2003. With a budget of just £1,000 to buy and restore their Mini, Mike turned to the classified ads to find a suitable car, and first to be inspected was a P-registered Mini Clubman. The condition was OK but there was rust to deal with, and at £750 it was just too expensive. Next up was an Almond Green 1968 model, and although it clearly needed work it had potential, which was enough for Mike to pay just £300. OK, so it looked a bit tired, the paintwork was a mess and the interior was a bit tatty, but the test drive revealed a car that went well, with the engine, gearbox, brakes and steering all giving Mike confidence that he'd found the perfect car for Edd to work his magic.

Jobs to be tackled

Despite being in very original condition and with minimal signs of serious corrosion underneath – although on closer investigation back at the workshop it turned out to be worse than they thought – there were some major paintwork and rust issues to deal with on the surface. The Mini would eventually get a full respray, but before that there was rusty bodywork to sort. Both jobs involved hours of preparation, getting the body ready for the corrosion repairs and for the new paintwork. The engine bay also came in for attention, with some key parts smartened up with new paint. So Edd certainly had his work cut out. Here's what happened...

Every panel on old Minis needs checking for corrosion and Mike had already spotted a few problems.

Edd starts on the strip-down, making sure that any parts to be reused were carefully stored.

Bodywork – the preparation

With plenty of panel rot to deal with and a full respray on the cards, the first step in Edd's challenge was to prepare the bodywork for the work ahead – and that meant putting in the hours in the workshop and stripping the little Mini of all its exterior trim and fittings, not to mention a few panels. It was certainly fiddly and tedious work, but, as he would tell you, it was important that it was approached carefully and methodically if the finished car was to meet the high standards of *Wheeler Dealers*, and careful preparation early on would pay dividends later in the project. There was to be no rushing of this stage, so it was out with the toolbox and time to tackle that unloved bodywork.

Exterior trim and fittings

He got started by removing all of the lights and brightwork, taking care not to damage these nice original fixtures. They could always be replaced with new parts – one of the plus points of the Mini is its fantastic parts availability – but, with originality important to the project, careful removal was the order of the day. With only a simple toolkit needed

for these jobs it was out with the screwdriver to remove the two screws securing the indicator side repeaters to the front wings, and then remove the front indicator lenses – glass items rather than plastic on this early Mini, and being such lovely period parts he certainly didn't want to damage them. Carefully removing the bezel and then releasing the lens from the rubber seal saw them off the car and safely stored away.

The headlamps were next, first removing the chrome bezels, which were secured to the lamp with a small screw, before undoing the lamp retaining screws and disconnecting the wiring at the back. Then, with the bonnet raised, the 'wavy' chrome grille was unscrewed. This was quickly followed by unbolting the bumpers, unscrewing and removing the front number plate, and carefully prising the Austin badge from the bonnet. The last jobs were levering off the wiper arms, removing the door handles and unscrewing the rear light lenses – retained by two crosshead screws at the top and one at the bottom – and removing the light units themselves.

Throughout this stage Edd was assessing the condition of each part to see if renovation

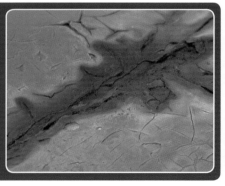
A full respray would sort the badly blistered paintwork but it would mean hours of prep for Edd.

The 'wavy' grille marks this out as an early model, but it's easy to source replacement parts for the Mini.

More stripping down. Take care with delicate plastic parts like these as they are easily damaged.

How much did it cost?

Car	£300
Materials	£30
Panels	£80
Paint	£150
Respray	£400
Trim parts	£140
Total	**£1,100**

or renewal would be required (though plenty of companies out there are able to restore chrome parts to as-new condition Edd knew it wasn't always the cheapest option, so he had to consider whether replacing them with new items would be more cost-effective). In the end a new grille and bumpers were added to the parts list while a bit of elbow grease would see other bits looking as good as new; so the latter were saved and carefully stored to prevent damage and to avoid losing vital screws and clips – something all too easily done, and very annoying when it comes to reassembly.

with a new part. As ever when restoring a classic car there was the potential to find other problems as you go along, and that would be the case with the Mini. Removing the petrol tank from the boot – he emptied it first to make the job easier and then disconnected the fuel hoses and wiring – he discovered that water had got in and caused the boot floor to rot away beneath the tank, so that would be another job on the list before the little car got back on the road.

Body panels

Next up for the show's master mechanic was removing some of the panels – these would be resprayed separately, so removing them at this stage not only made sense but would also allow easier access when it came to doing other jobs. Despite its tatty appearance the bonnet was in good condition and it took only a few moments with the socket set to unbolt it from the hinges; but unfortunately the boot lid was just too far gone, so Edd took the decision to replace this

Glass panels

With the strip-down progressing well Edd turned his attention to removing the glass, starting with the front and rear screens. His first job was to carefully remove the chrome beading – not easy, as it was old and brittle and might easily crack, which (of course) was exactly what happened. It was not a problem in this case, though, as new ones could be sourced which would look much better anyway when matched to the shiny new paint that would be applied later.

Another classic rust trap is below the boot-mounted fuel tank, and this one had succumbed.

Edd managed to crack the chrome windscreen beading – it's easily damaged – but new ones would be fitted.

A special tool aids windscreen removal but stout gloves and goggles are sensible in case of breakage.

The rubber seals were next, and, working from inside the car, a special tool that's designed for the task (although a screwdriver would have worked too, he told us) was used to prise the seal from the bodywork, carefully pushing the screen out a section at a time. He took extra care not to break the glass as it was removed, as not only would this have added to the parts bill – not good news when they were working with such a tight budget, and sure to bring disapproval from Mike – but it might also prove potentially dangerous; so heavy-duty gloves and eye protection were Edd's safety tip when tackling this sort of job. Fortunately the rear side windows were much easier to remove, being held in place by just a couple of screws at the B-pillar with two more securing the release catch at the rear. The sliding front windows would prove a bit trickier, held in

place by various screws that were almost certain to be rusted in place, so the sensible decision was taken to just leave them in position and carefully mask them ready for the trip to the paint shop.

Assessing the bodyshell

By now the Mini was looking very different to when it first arrived in the workshop, and with all of these parts removed Edd began by investigating the true state of the bodywork. It was becoming clear that extensive rust repairs were going to be needed, but just how bad was it? He was about to find out in the next stage of the project.

Donning a mask and goggles, Edd set to work with an orbital sander to discover the extent of the rust repairs that would be required. The paint was removed around local areas of corrosion in the front wings first, starting with the headlamps and then working back to the scuttle. Luckily neither of these areas was suffering from serious rot so the application of some rust-remedy and filler soon had them ready for painting. More of a problem was the A-panel on the passenger side – a common rot-spot on Minis – so he set to work using a screwdriver to dislodge loose pieces of rusty metal followed by more sanding, which exposed an area that was in need of major attention.

Next up was the passenger door and rear wing, where blistered paint provided evidence that more

▼ The S badge on the back of this Cooper model denoted extra power, up to 70bhp in 1071cc form.

The first stage in preparing the bodywork – tackling areas of localised rust.

Larger areas need a sander but care is needed to prevent damage to otherwise sound metalwork.

The old filler had to go, otherwise it would ruin the finished respray.

An orbital sander is the easiest way to remove old paint so that the damage can be properly assessed.

Filling the dent was the only answer for the door, but ensure that the filler and hardener are mixed properly.

work was almost certainly going to be needed. Sure enough, sanding the door back to bare metal revealed a large dent that had been carelessly filled, not to mention bodged with some plasticine-like material that was now falling out. This was an area that was going to need proper repairs before the Mini could head to the paint shop.

Bodywork – the repairs

Repairing the door

As Edd himself told us, preparing a panel for repairs is a bit tedious but is a vital step if you want to do a job properly. Trying to save time here would only result in a poor job and the chance that problems could reappear later, spoiling the nice new paintwork.

With all of the paint removed and the damage exposed, every last trace of old filler was sanded away so that the original dent could be tackled. It turned out to be quite major too, so rather than just use lots of filler Edd opted to attempt knocking out the dent from the rear of the panel – access was easy thanks to the Mini's simple construction. It's here that a proper 'shrinking hammer' would have been useful – it's designed to compress and gently twist the metal as you hammer, helping to return stretched metal to its original shape. Unfortunately he didn't have one and the metal had stretched quite badly, so with the size of the dent reduced a bit there was no choice but to apply filler. Ensuring it was properly mixed according to the instructions – normally a golf-ball sized blob of filler to a pea-sized blob of hardener (but he recommends checking before you start work) – thin layers were applied and smoothed using a flat edge before being left to dry.

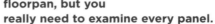

That wasn't the end of the job, though, as more preparation was going to be needed, so while the filler was hardening Edd removed the door completely, which would make the next stage much easier. It came off easily, just a couple of nuts securing it to the hinge. Laying the door down flat meant he could rub back the whole panel, using an orbital sander to carefully smooth any minor bumps and imperfections from the filler so that the door would be ready for priming. An aerosol can of primer did the job nicely, and the newly repaired door was all ready for its trip to the paint shop. While he had the can of primer in his hand, Edd applied a quick layer to the front wing and scuttle panel as well.

Replacing the A-panel

This was always going to be the trickiest job on the old Mini, and Edd was going to need all of his skills and experience if he was going to achieve a top-class finish. Knowing Mike would accept nothing less, the pressure was on!

Before work could start properly there was a bit of preparation needed that would make the job a bit easier, the first thing being to remove the nearside front wheel. With the Mini securely mounted on axle stands, getting the wheel out of the way gave Edd clear access to the wheel arch and the end of the sill where repairs were going to be needed. The next job was to carefully prise away the gutter trim covering the seam running down the A-pillar to the top of the wheel arch. A suitable tool was used to prevent damage as this part was in good condition and would be cleaned up and replaced before painting.

The lower door hinge was next to come off, a couple of bolts at the rear of the A-panel being all that needed undoing. With all of those parts out of

Buying one

➔ **Rust is the biggest problem with older Minis. Rot-spots include the inner and outer wings, sills and floorpan, but you really need to examine every panel.**

➔ **The A-series engine is easy to rebuild, but it's prone to oil leaks and you need to watch for low oil pressure, smoke from the exhaust and a tired cooling system.**

➔ **Watch for excessive noise from the gearbox and jumping out of gear. It shares its oil with the engine, so regular oil and filter changes aid longevity.**

➔ **The interior couldn't be simpler, so even if it's tatty you'll have no trouble getting replacement trim. Parts are cheap, too.**

➔ **Originality is an important factor on early cars, so speak to experts about the right specification for the year. It's easy to harm the value by fitting the wrong parts.**

With the filler sanded down, a coat of primer readies the door for the paint shop.

Rotten A-panels are a classic Mini problem but cheap repair sections are available if you're handy with a welder.

the way Edd could set about discovering the extent of the rusty metal, and the first job was deciding exactly how much would need to be cut out. Using an engineer's square and a suitable scribe the old exterior panel was marked to assist with cutting; an angle grinder was then used to carefully cut away the rotten section (the same markings would be used to cut the repair panel to shape). Careful marking and measuring at this stage would also ensure that the replacement panel would fit perfectly, saving a lot of time and effort later on. Unfortunately the exploration work also revealed that rot had attacked the inner panel so this too got the cutting treatment; and he found that a new section would be needed at the end of the sill. But with all of the frilly metal removed – carefully, as rusty metal can be very sharp – Edd set about getting the new sections in place.

The first job was to offer up the repair panel for a trial fit – it looked good at this stage and was held in place with suitably positioned G-clamps. The lower door hinge was bolted back into place, and then the passenger door was replaced in its aperture and secured using more G-clamps. It seemed like a lot of effort, but Edd wanted to make absolutely sure

Removing the gutter trim needed care as it was going to be reused.

that the A-panel repair section lined up perfectly with adjacent panels, as it would be too late to alter things once it was welded in place. A handy safety tip was the order of the day first, though, Edd recommending you check that your protective mask is suitable for MIG welding, as the light is a lot brighter than gas welding. It was excellent advice as always from the workshop maestro.

Then, on with the job. With just a minor bit of fettling needed the new section was a perfect fit, so it was out with the MIG welder to tack it into place. And with the section securely in position he finished

▶ The interior couldn't be simpler, meaning you can just concentrate on enjoying the driving experience.

▶ The Cooper and Cooper S models fetch much higher prices, but fakes are rife so you need to be wary when buying one.

Only the lower section of the repair panel was going to be needed, as Edd finds out.

Measure twice, cut once is Edd's motto, as you don't want to remove healthy metal.

It's important to assess things as you go, so only cut out small areas at a time.

Further trial fitting is vital to ensure everything lines up. It'll be too late after welding!

One of Edd's handy tips is using a paper template to help measure new metal.

Use a welding magnet to hold repair sections in place, as Edd has done here.

Preparation for painting is time-consuming but important if you want a perfect finish.

Bare metal needs acid etch primer to help the new paint adhere.

applying the continuous weld along the seams between old and new panels.

With a new section of metal let-in at the rear of the wheel arch where the A-panel meets the sill, all that was left was to weld in a small triangle of metal at the base of the A-panel. For this small job, Edd used the trusty method of making a paper template first, a dirty finger being enough to trace the outline of the hole on to the paper before transferring the outline to a fresh sheet of steel. A pair of metal cutters soon had a replacement piece ready, which was held in place on the body using a welder's magnet. These handy items are easy to source from welding suppliers, and come in a variety of shapes and angles – perfect for locating new metalwork in tricky areas. Once the new piece was MIG welded into place, the A-panel repair was finished and the Mini was almost ready for the next stage.

Paintwork

Preparation

As with many tasks when restoring a classic car, careful preparation was vital in producing a finish to be proud of, and as only the best would do for *Wheeler Dealers* Edd still had many hours of work ahead before the Mini would head off to the paint shop. And as he'll tell you, plenty of money can be saved if you're willing to do the detailed preparation yourself.

The major areas of cracked and blistered paintwork had already been sanded back, so the next job now was to tackle all of the exposed areas of bare metal. Edd starting by rubbing these down to a smooth finish, and then applying a coat of acid etch primer that helped any subsequent paint layers adhere to the metal. Once that was dry traditional grey primer was applied with an aerosol can before rubbing it down with 800-grade wet-and-dry paper to achieve a perfectly smooth surface. A sanding block was a handy tool here, especially for larger areas, as it helped in applying even pressure to the surface. Areas of the bodywork where the existing paint was in reasonable condition were just rubbed with an abrasive pad to provide a 'key' for the new paint to adhere to.

Then it was on to the masking stage. Even Edd admitted that it was a bit of a tedious process, but

BEHIND THE SCENES

The Mini was amongst the first cars that Mike and Edd tackled, and they were only just beginning to discover what a steep learning curve lay ahead of them before the show would become the success it is today. First of all they were working with a tiny budget, so buying a suitable project car wasn't easy. In fact, with time running out Mike had no choice but to buy this Mini, and while it was obvious that all was not well – the problems with panel rust and poor paintwork were easy to see – it was actually quite a lot worse underneath. Not only was there the rotten boot floor mentioned earlier, but the rear suspension mountings had succumbed to serious corrosion. But there was no time to find an alternative, so Mike had to ignore the problems and buy the car anyway. There would be an awful lot of extra work to tackle off-camera, and plenty of late nights.

And working on the car wasn't going to be trouble-free either. First of all – and despite his skills with the spanners – Edd wasn't given much time to learn about the art of paint preparation and repairs, all while being filmed. And with the crew still getting to grips with the difficulties involved in filming the restoration of a classic car, it soon became clear that the dust created by sanding paintwork and filler would play havoc with the delicate equipment they were using. Challenging? You bet...

it is another job where attention to detail is vital before a car enters the spray booth. Protecting mechanical and interior parts from overspray not only prevented damage but also meant not having to spend time later removing excess paint from places it shouldn't have reached. And rather than resort to tatty old pieces of newspaper, Edd advised buying large rolls of paper along with rolls of masking tape – cheap, and ideal for the job. Every aperture had to be carefully masked, and he didn't forget the small areas that could easily have been missed, such as winding tape

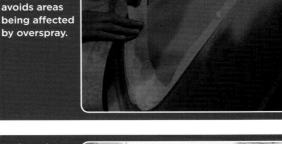

Masking is another time-consuming job, but it avoids areas being affected by overspray.

Don't rush the masking-up. It might be tedious but it'll save a lot of time and effort later.

In the paint booth, Edd uses panel wipe to rid the surface of grease and contaminants.

The new parts can go back on, the new grille really setting off that classic Mini face.

It can be cheaper to replace parts than re-chrome originals; be careful not to damage the soft new paint.

around the windscreen wiper spindles. It was all about attention to detail, and there were just two jobs remaining before the glossy new paint could be applied. The first was to carefully wipe every panel with the solution known as 'pre-paint' or 'panel wipe' – stuff that Edd used frequently in any episodes where paintwork was involved – which helped to remove any contaminants such as dirt and grease from the metal surfaces. Forgetting this stage would have caused problems when the paint was applied, spoiling the top-class finish the boys were aiming for. And last but not least was running a 'tack cloth' over the panels, a sticky cloth that would pick up any tiny particles of dust that remained on the surface.

The Mini is definitely one of my all-time favourite classics, and is just such good fun to drive. I know it's a bit of a cliché but it really does handle like a go-kart, and you can chuck it around a twisty road without having to drive at the sort of speeds that'll risk your licence. If you want a small classic that'll be easy to work on, this is definitely the car for you; and there's a great owners' scene too, so you'll never be stuck for help or advice. Mind you, as I found out for myself with the one we restored on the show, there are a few things to watch out for!

The new paint

By the time the Mini reached this stage, the spending had been modest – just £30 on preparation materials and £45 on the A-panel repair section – so there was plenty left in the kitty. But Edd had really put the hours in, repairing the rust and preparing the bodywork for its new coat of paint, and all that work was about to pay off.

For the respray, Mike and Edd chose to have the Mini painted in its original green colour, but this time it would be modern 'two-pack' paint that was applied. It was dangerous stuff, though, containing harmful chemicals such as isocyanates, so Edd's advice was to either be very careful and take proper precautions (using the correct protective masks and the like) or, better still, do what he did and employ the services of a professional sprayer.

All of the effort had paid off, because the little Mini looked fantastic when it arrived back at the workshop. The next stage was refitting all of the panels and trim.

Refitting

Tempting as it was to rush through this stage to get the car finished, Edd knew that patience was needed so that every detail would be just right.

Care was also needed as the glass and exterior trim were refitted – the fresh paintwork was still quite soft, and it would be easy to damage it as the parts were screwed in place. Most of the original parts would be reused, but the little Mini did get a new boot lid to replace the rotten part Edd had taken off, and there would be a new grille, bumpers and door mirrors, as they were cheaper than getting the pitted and slightly corroded originals renovated.

And it was at this stage that Edd's methodical approach to the strip-down paid dividends. All of the clips and fittings had been carefully stored and the wires for the lighting had been labelled so he knew exactly what went where, and that was more helpful advice for this stage. Also, taking plenty of pictures during the removal process acted as a reminder when the time came for reassembly, and he tested the electrics as he went along – that way, if he discovered any problems it would save having to dismantle components again. More top tips!

▲ Reckoned to be the rarest of all the early Minis, this pristine Almond Green 1962 Austin Super Seven still wears the original tax disc from December 1962!

The engine bay

With all of the exterior trim parts refitted the Mini was almost finished, but there was just time to tackle a few last jobs under the bonnet. Things were looking a bit tatty, and if Mike was to get the best price when it came to sell then every part of the car had to look its best, and that included the engine bay.

Smartening the engine bay really lifts the appearance, but Edd gives it a thorough de-greasing first.

For the best finish remove any surface rust from parts with a sander or wet-and-dry paper.

Using a brush is not the best solution but it saved time and effort, and the results still looked good.

A coat of satin black paint is a cheap way to smarten up any tatty engine parts.

The first job was to see what was needed, and that meant a thorough degreasing was required. Edd used a proprietary engine degreasing solution applied from a spray can and then brushed into all of the engine's nooks and crevices, before being cleaned off with water from a hose. Despite the Mini's basic electrical system precautions were still taken to cover any major ignition parts to save them from a thorough drenching; even more care needs to be taken if you are dealing with a modern motor with its delicate, ECU-controlled electronics. The Mini, however, was straightforward, and with the engine cleaned up Edd was able to assess the areas in need of some renovation, identifying the ignition coil, the rocker cover and the air cleaner housing as parts that were about to benefit from some fresh paint.

Using a grinder or wet-and-dry paper it was easy to get rid of the old paint and any surface corrosion before applying a layer of acid etch primer and then grey primer. Then the parts got two coats of satin black for a smart, modern finish. But that wasn't the end of the job, as the engine block got a fresh coat of black enamel paint while the radiator's header tank also got the enamel treatment. The latter would have been better sprayed but that would have meant masking the area, so applying the paint by brush was easier. As Edd himself said, some owners spend many, many hours on 'dressing' an engine bay to get it looking perfect, but the finished job here still looked smart, giving the engine bay a new lease of life.

Just two jobs remained. A new set of HT leads were fitted to replace the tired-looking originals – though Edd did advise that a minor service might also be considered, if necessary – and then the bonnet could finally be refitted. It bolted into

A quick service, including new HT leads, ensures the Mini runs as well as it looks.

Panels like the bonnet might need adjustment for refitting, but it's worth getting the shut lines just right.

Doesn't it look great? You'd never know it was that same tatty car that Mike bought for just £300.

place easily, though some adjustment was needed to obtain a perfect fit. Nice neat shut lines on a panel showed that the job had been done properly, and it would have been a shame to spoil this fantastic restoration at the last minute.

Job done

And that was it – the Mini was finished! Mike and Edd had taken a tired but relatively solid example of this iconic small car and turned it into a classic to be proud of. It had taken plenty of hours in the workshop, cutting out the rot and welding in solid metal, and preparing the car for a superb respray, but the effort had been worth it. The Mini looked superb, and all that was left was for Mike to do what he does best and find a new owner. And that owner was a man who had come all the way from Guernsey to get his hands on a piece of *Wheeler*

Dealers restoration magic. How much did he pay? A bargain £1,300.

Final test drive

Where better to take this iconic British car than into the perfect habitat, the English countryside. Mike jumped behind the wheel, and in his own words he was gobsmacked by the transformation. Edd had done an amazing job. Not only was the Mini looking fantastic but it drove beautifully too. As Mike himself told us, this car was a slice of motoring history and it was one that would put a smile on the face of passers-by whenever they saw it. And you couldn't really ask for more than that with this stunning restoration.

A job well done.

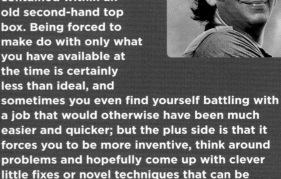

The Mini is a great car to work on, and while the tight packaging can make reaching some components a bit of a squeeze, the engineering is pretty basic, so it's perfect for the DIY mechanic. In fact it's probably the perfect car to learn about restoration skills. Not only is just about every part available but there's plenty of opportunity to undertake a few modifications and perhaps improve the performance. It's a car that responds really well to tuning. The other great thing is that most parts are really cheap, so restoring one won't break the bank.

Having said that, being the first series of the show meant everything was a bit of an adventure. Even though I had been playing around with cars for quite some time, by then my tool kit was pretty meagre and was contained within an old second-hand top box. Being forced to make do with only what you have available at the time is certainly less than ideal, and sometimes you even find yourself battling with a job that would otherwise have been much easier and quicker; but the plus side is that it forces you to be more inventive, think around problems and hopefully come up with clever little fixes or novel techniques that can be shared with others.

Jaguar E-Type

Enzo Ferrari was a man who knew more than most about producing achingly gorgeous cars, so when he reputedly called the E-Type 'the most beautiful car ever made', you knew you were in the presence of something special. The new Jaguar was launched in 1961 to critical acclaim, its styling appearing other-worldly compared to the dull saloons of the day, and it's a car that remains just as admired today – and very sought-after, if the spiralling prices are anything to go by.

Getting one into the *Wheeler Dealers* workshop was going to make for a very special project, then, but with prices of early cars putting them out of reach Mike's search focused on the later Series 3. With a budget of just £15,000 the hunt was on for one of these big V12s, and there was one car that caught his eye early on.

Obviously he was well aware of the risks associated with buying a cheap E-Type, but this one looked good and the price was right, so he was straight on the phone to the owner to arrange a viewing. He wasn't disappointed either, the big cat turning out to be a very solid example, with no rust or damage in key areas such as the wings, sills, or floorpan. The engine was strong too, and the car felt good on the test drive. It was a car that Mike just had to have. Not that it was entirely problem-free – Edd would need some work to do, after all: attention was needed to the bodywork and interior, and there were a few mechanical tasks to do as well. But it was nothing the top mechanic couldn't handle, and after some tough negotiating Mike secured the wonderful Jag for £13,250. There could be big profits... if everything went well.

Jobs to be tackled

The E-Type had to look perfect if it was to fetch big money, so the biggest task facing Edd was sorting a few bodywork issues. The huge, complex bonnet had suffered damage to the lower air intake, so that would have to be sorted, and the nasty black stone-chip paint that had been applied to the sills would have to go as well. There were more cosmetic issues to be tackled too, including refurbishing the wire wheels and refreshing the tired interior. Mechanical jobs required included fixing an oil leak from the differential and replacing the battered exhaust system. A fundamentally solid example it may have been, but it wouldn't have been a proper *Wheeler Dealers* project if there wasn't still plenty to do before the Jaguar was ready for sale.

The damaged air scoop was letting the side down so Edd splashed out £600 on a new panel.

The corroded bonnet hinge plates were a serious problem, but thankfully the new repair panel would sort these.

Repairing the bonnet

Preparation

The damage to the bonnet's lower air scoop was letting down the car's looks, so that was the first job needing attention. After close examination it was clear that a straightforward repair wasn't going to be possible as the scoop beneath the bumper was too badly damaged and corroded, so a replacement was the only option. Edd also discovered a dent close to the nearside indicator, and, more worryingly, some nasty corrosion around the bonnet hinge panels where they attached to the chassis brackets. Bodywork repairs on these cars could prove both tricky and very expensive – a complete replacement could cost thousands of pounds. Fortunately, however, the E-Type's bonnet was constructed from around 13 separate sections, so replacing just the lower intake section would effectively fix all of the issues in one go.

But first the bonnet needed to be removed, and this needed to be done carefully to avoid any further damage to the large and unwieldy panel. A second pair of hands was definitely useful here. The hinges were easy to unbolt, and then it was a matter of disconnecting the wiring plug for the headlights and separate indicators/sidelights, and disconnecting the supporting gas strut. So far so good. But Edd had a clever plan to make removing the bonnet a bit easier. With the bonnet opened fully, the ramp was lowered until the whole unit was sitting securely on the bumper overriders, and with things nice and stable all that was needed was to remove the hinge pins. He expected these to be fixed very firmly in place, and they were, but the liberal application of penetrating fluid helped

free things up and a strong pair of grips were used to extract them. With Paul's help the bonnet could be carefully lifted clear of the car.

Removing the damaged air-scoop was the next task, so Edd got to work with the socket set and screwdriver, removing the grille and bumper. The chrome-work was carefully stored out of harm's way – it was important to avoid damage to parts like these, as refurbishment would be costly. The light units were next but were easily removed – just two screws secured the indicator and sidelight lenses, with a further four screws attaching the light unit to the bonnet panel itself, and then the wiring was gently pulled through. The side panels around the rusty hinge plates would prove more of a struggle, however, as the securing bolts were hidden behind layers of underseal and accumulated muck, and a bit of elbow grease was required before they could be accessed. With that done it turned out that the fixings themselves weren't too badly corroded, so all of the various screws and bolts were undone and the side panels and air scoop carefully prised from the bonnet, using a flat blade. This last stage took

Separating the lower section from the bonnet was the first job, and involved some careful levering.

They came apart easily enough, though, and the bonnet needed minimal preparation prior to fitting the new panel.

How much did it cost?

Car	£13,250
Bonnet panel	£665
Wheel refurbishment	£200
Paintwork	£900
Interior re-trim	£400
Exhaust system	£600
Service items	£75
Total	*£16,090*

patience and a careful approach, though, as it was important not to damage the rest of the bonnet. Edd certainly didn't need any more work on this challenging project!

Fitting the new section and refitting the bonnet

Buying the complete lower panel, which included the air scoop and all-important hinge panels, had left a £600 hole in the budget, but it was money well spent if Mike and Edd were to do the E-Type justice. With the adjoining seams of the bonnet cleaned of any remaining paint and sealant it was a straightforward job to bolt the new section into place, and thanks to buying a good quality part it fitted perfectly. Edd also reused many of the old fixings, as they were perfectly serviceable – a useful tip for helping to keep the parts spend on a restoration as low as possible. The exterior trim would be refitted later once the car had returned from the paint shop. In the meantime there was a another handy tip for refitting the wiring loom for the lights: attaching a length of old Bowden cable (a speedometer cable or brake cable from a bicycle is perfect) to the end of the wiring loom made feeding it through the bonnet apertures a simple task.

Reuniting the bonnet with the rest of the car would be a two-man task, so again Paul was drafted in to help. As Edd explained, it could be quite a tricky job. The hand-built nature of these cars meant that panel alignment could differ from car to car, so getting the perfect fit took patience, and it was important that the bonnet didn't strike the ground when it was opened.

With the new aluminium hinge brackets bolted to the chassis, the bonnet was attached with the bolts just hand-tight – careful adjustment of the hinges was needed, but once properly aligned the bolts were tightened, the hinge pins tapped back into position and the support strut refitted. After a trip to the paint shop the big Jag would be looking

With the new section in place the wiring for the lights could be reconnected. Note the helpful labels.

It's a two-man job replacing that expensive bonnet, and a bit of fettling was needed to align the hinges.

Mike took the wire wheels to a specialist to be refurbished with new spokes; they did a superb job.

better than ever, but before those badly painted sills were tackled there was the matter of some mechanical work.

Refurbishing the wire wheels

While Edd was hard at work, Mike was on the road on his way to a specialist who would get the gorgeous wire wheels looking as good as new. They weren't in bad shape considering the car's age, but quite a few of the spokes had corroded and the wheels needed a thorough clean. The Series 3 E-Type was fitted with steel wheels and chrome hubcaps as standard, but it wasn't uncommon to find the optional wire wheels fitted, and while they look terrific they can need refurbishment. Thankfully there are plenty of specialists that can do the job, and the one Mike chose employed traditional techniques to restore them.

First the rusty spokes were cut out and brand new ones formed from metal blanks. Once screwed into place, the spokes were adjusted to ensure the rim of each wheel was perfectly aligned, and at just £200 for all four wheels this was to prove something of a bargain. Mike even helped in their restoration, for a nice personal touch.

Locating and fixing a differential oil leak

The E-Type was about to be treated to a brand new exhaust system, but as Edd began to remove the old system he was in for a nasty shock. In fact he'd found a problem that in his own words 'made his blood run cold'. Working at the back of the car to prepare for replacing the exhaust he noticed oil coating the bottom of the differential. This was bad news. Not only might it involve a difficult and

Buying one

➜ The complex construction and corrosion issues mean an expert inspection is vital. And check the condition of the chrome and Mazak exterior trim, as replacement is pricey. Restoration costs can be eye-watering – so, you've been warned.

➜ The V12 engine is thirsty and not exactly DIY-friendly. Watch for oil and coolant leaks, signs of overheating and head gasket failure, low oil pressure, and rough running due to ignition or carburettor issues.

➜ There's a choice of manual or automatic gearboxes. Check they feel and sound healthy on the test drive. Differential oils leaks are labour-intensive to cure and can affect the inboard rear brakes.

➜ Worn brakes and suspension can be costly to sort. If wire wheels have been fitted, check the condition of the spokes, splines and hubs.

➜ The interior used quality materials and a retrim is expensive, so check the condition carefully. Ancient wiring can cause problems too, so check it all works.

The oil leak from the differential made Edd's blood run cold, the fix involving a lot of labour time.

labour-intensive fix, but it could also prove costly, putting more pressure on an already tight budget. Closer examination revealed that the leak seemed to be coming from the nose of the differential where the propshaft enters the unit, so it wasn't going to be a quick fix. Edd had no choice but to completely remove the differential and replace the failed oil seal.

Removing the differential

Though this wasn't going to be an easy job, Edd had a clever plan. On the E-Type, and indeed on many Jaguars of the time, the differential and suspension were attached to a subframe (an arrangement that would form the basis of many a custom car and hot rod). If this entire subframe could be dropped from the car, the differential could be reached and the oil seal replaced. It was a fairly daunting task even for someone as experienced as Edd, and access was awkward. It was a job that would require a lot of patience and penetrating fluid.

There were plenty of parts to remove and disconnect, so the first job was to undo the bolts that attached the suspension's radius arms to the

Some dismantling was involved before the differential could be accessed. This is one of the suspension radius arm bolts.

▲ This earlier E-Type shows the purity of line that attracted so much admiration when the car was launched way back in 1961.

chassis. The brake hydraulic pipes were next to be disconnected, and with that done the bolts securing the propshaft to the differential pinion shaft could be undone. The handbrake mechanism was disconnected – a fiddly job – and, with the whole unit supported using a transmission jack, the four bolts each side that secured the subframe to the chassis were then removed.

With the subframe and differential sitting securely on a sturdy tool cabinet, the car was carefully raised on the ramp – taking it a stage at a time to ensure that nothing had been left connected by mistake – to separate the two parts. It's a heavy item, so getting help was certainly a good idea, but with the subframe free Edd could get on with replacing that leaking seal.

Replacing the oil seal

The first task was to remove the input pinion flange nut, and Edd employed a handy tip to assist with refitting. Since it was important that the nut was replaced in exactly the same position, before it was

Edd had a clever idea for removing the rear subframe. Just four bolts each side attach it to the body.

The subframe came away as planned so now it was on with curing that oil leak.

This flange on the front of the differential was removed to gain access to the leaking oil seal.

Here's the cause of the leak. Edd resorted to a chisel to remove the old seal.

The new seal was cheap to buy and after a soak in oil it was gently tapped into place.

Carefully marking the flange bolt and thread helps ensure it's tightened correctly.

unscrewed he used a punch to carefully mark both the nut and the thread. The handbrake levers would prove a handy way to prevent the pinion from rotating as the nut was unscrewed, so with these firmly gripped the nut was undone and the input flange removed.

Removing the actual seal was the next challenge, as the usual methods for such a job wouldn't work in this case. Edd didn't have a suitable puller handy, and packing the area with grease to force the seal out wouldn't work either, as the grease would just end up in the differential – not good news. So it was out with the hammer and chisel, and with some careful and patient work the seal was removed.

Edd had sensibly left the new seal soaking in oil for a few hours to ensure it was completely lubricated and prevent future wear, so the excess oil just needed to be wiped away and the seal was ready for fitting. With the new gasket in place, the largest socket in the toolbox – a 50mm one – was employed so that even pressure could be applied to tap the new seal into position, Edd listening for the change in sound that indicated that it was fully home in the nose of the differential. Once seated correctly the input flange could be replaced and the nut done up, ensuring it aligned with the marks made previously.

All that was left was to bolt the subframe back on to the car and reconnect all of the suspension and brake components. As Edd himself said, it wasn't the easiest of jobs to undertake – access to some components was limited and there were a few corroded fittings to deal with – but it was manageable, and given that you wouldn't want to do it very often it could even be a good opportunity to upgrade the brakes and differential. Sound advice as always.

The very last job was bleeding the brakes – remember, the hydraulic pipework had been

disconnected to remove the subframe – but the design of the E-Type meant a slightly different approach was needed. Rather than the rear disc brakes being mounted on the wheel hubs, as with most cars, they were mounted inboard next to the differential, so there was a novel way of accessing the brake calipers in order to attach the hose to the bleed nipples. They were reached from inside the cabin, so the first job was to remove the rear seat revealing two access panels, one for each brake. With these unbolted, the hose could be attached to the calipers and the brakes bled in the normal way. With all of the air removed, and the brake pedal nice and firm, the job was finished; but while it hadn't been expensive, it had taken up a lot of extra time. And there was plenty more work still to do, so time to press ahead.

Assessing and replacing the exhaust system

One of the problems Mike had noticed when first viewing the car had been the crooked and slightly tatty exhaust 'fantail', the tailpipe exit that's a unique styling point on some E-Types. It

With the subframe refitted, it was just a case of bleeding the brakes. The inboard rear calipers are accessed from the cabin.

The crooked fantail was tatty as well, so a new one would be needed.

▲ The 4.2-litre engine in this version is less complex than the V12 that Mike bought. Note the separate exhaust pipes rather than the fantail of the project car.

The damaged exhaust system was leaking and not good enough for this iconic classic, so it had to go.

An E-Type exhaust is a hefty item so another pair of hands is always useful.

Fitting the new exhaust was straight-forward, Edd using exhaust paste to seal the joints.

The new fantail looks superb and finishes the job nicely.

The E-Type is an amazing car, and although I haven't always been sold on the looks I must admit that working on one changed my mind. They are complex, though, and the thought of carrying out major work can be daunting. However, it proved easier than I expected to work on, and it was made easier by the fantastic parts availability. Having said that, the hand-built nature of these cars can make things a bit trickier – you have to be prepared for some extra fettling, and some jobs can put up a fight; in addition the complication of that V12 engine probably makes a six-cylinder car a better bet. But having had one in the workshop, I can really appreciate the engineering that went into them, and it's easy to see why so many people love them.

was spoiling the look of this wonderful classic, but it looked like a quick replacement would have things looking as good as new. However, as always it wasn't going to be quite that simple...

With the car at the workshop and up on the ramp Edd could investigate further, and what he found was about to add yet more expense to the growing parts bill. It wasn't just the fantail that needed sorting – the entire exhaust system was looking past its best, with dented pipework, corrosion and leaks from the rear silencer. There was nothing for it but to dig into the kitty and buy a complete new stainless-steel system.

Despite being big and very heavy, removing the old system wasn't too difficult, although using a transmission jack to support it made the job a bit easier. A spray of penetrating fluid ensured that the bolts connecting the various joints in the system came undone easily, and with the nuts securing the downpipes to the exhaust manifold undone and the hangers released it was soon removed from the car with a hand from Paul. In fact it was a good demonstration of the need for assistance with some jobs during a restoration.

◀ Roadsters were just as beautiful as the coupé, and they fetch big money nowadays.

Not all classics are as complex or as large as an E-Type, of course, but don't be afraid to get some help with tasks like these, as it will make the job safer and easier.

Edd had spent £600 on the new stainless-steel system, but it was a quality part that would last for many years, and with exhaust paste applied to the various joints to aid sealing everything went back together without any problems. The finishing touch was a brand new chrome fantail that was easily fitted, and the E-Type now sounded as good as it looked.

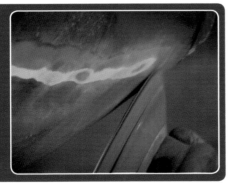

The stone-chip paint on the sills was sanded back. Thankfully there was no corrosion hidden beneath.

Preparing the sills

An obvious problem with the Jaguar was the paintwork on the sills. Instead of being in the correct body colour all the way to the bottom, a previous owner had applied some form of stone-chip protection. And while it might have protected the bodywork it looked neither attractive nor original, so it had to go.

Wearing suitable protection in the form of goggles and ear defenders, Edd set to work with the orbital sander, starting by rubbing away the worst of the old material to give a nice smooth surface. More important was to remove the 'lip' between the original paintwork and the stone-chip, as the aim was to end up with a nice even finish once the new paint was applied. There was a concern that removing the old protection might reveal corrosion beneath – always a possibility with old cars when someone might have applied thick layers of underseal to hide grotty metal and rot – but thankfully the Jaguar was solid, so with the area prepped it was off to the paint shop.

Applying the new paint

Nothing less than a perfect finish would do for this iconic car, so Edd chose to send it to the professionals to have the new air intake and the sills resprayed in their original 'Azure Blue'; and getting the job done properly meant achieving the perfect paint match. On a modern car, using the manufacturer's paint code would usually be enough for the correct match, but on older cars like these the paintwork has often faded, so it takes time to mix the right colour exactly so that the new paint blends in perfectly with the surrounding panels. A good area of paintwork was scanned and some clever mixing soon produced the perfect shade of blue. Once applied, the E-Type looked terrific and all ready for the finishing stages of the project.

All that was left on the outside was for Edd to refit all of the exterior trim and chrome-work, taking care not to damage the newly applied paint that would remain slightly soft until fully cured. The grille and front bumper were bolted into place; the indicator and sidelight units were screwed back on, followed by the lenses; and new chrome trim was fitted to the edge of the air intake to finish things off.

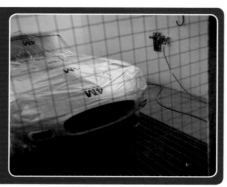
In the paint booth, ready for painting the new bonnet section and the sills. Only a professional job would do.

With the chrome trim refitted the bodywork was finished, and the big Jag was almost done.

Restoring leather trim

The charm of many older classics is their luxurious leather trim, but it can be expensive to restore. Nevertheless, don't ignore a particularly decrepit cabin – just make sure that the price is adjusted accordingly if it looks like a professional retrim may be needed. But if wear and damage isn't too extensive there are things you can do to bring it back to top condition. First off is a thorough clean – a soft sponge and warm soapy water will often do the trick in removing ingrained dirt. Pay attention to seams as well as the larger areas of leather, but don't use too much water as it can cause stitching to rot if it's not dried thoroughly. You can follow up with a mild solvent to remove final traces of grease and other contaminants. Light cracks can be filled, while faded and damaged areas can be re-coloured, either by hand or by spraying – there is a wide variety of products on the market designed to restore leather trim, so it's worth experimenting on a small area first to see which works best for you. It may take time and patience but it will be worth it, and once you've got back that original look don't forget to keep it in good condition with regular applications of hide food.

▲ This is the facia of an earlier roadster model. The layout is very similar to the project car, although there are fewer switches here.

Back from the re-trimmers the seats are in great condition and will really smarten up the interior.

The tatty door trims needed replacing. New ones weren't expensive and it's an easy job.

Retrimming the interior

With the paintwork and mechanical issues sorted, there was just one more job to be completed before the E-Type was ready to find a new owner. While the condition of the interior was basically sound – good news, as complete refurbishment would have been a costly business – it was a bit tatty in places, and that was never going to do for this most special of *Wheeler Dealers* projects. It was time for Edd to work more of his magic then.

The first job to tackle was the front seats, which were looking in need of light renovation. These were sent to a professional upholsterer to have some of the panels replaced, the threadbare side bolsters repaired and the rather saggy headrests plumped-up with new material. Just four bolts held each seat to the floorpan, and with these undone the chairs were easily removed. They would come back looking as good as new, with the repairs almost invisible, and would go a

With the seats bolted back in, the E-Type is finished and about to earn a healthy profit for the boys.

You're not going to be surprised to hear that I rate the E-Type as an absolute classic car icon. It's a gorgeous machine and I'm just as much a fan of them now as I was when I first saw one as a kid, so for me it was a car that we just had to have on *Wheeler Dealers*. Mind you, they aren't easy cars to buy, being complex and full of pitfalls that can cost a fortune to put right. If ever there was a car that needs expert advice before you take the plunge, this is it, and I was really happy to find the Series 3 car that we featured.

A budget of £15,000 wasn't that much for buying an E-Type, so the fact that I managed to get ours for such a good price was pretty amazing. We were pretty lucky too in that it wasn't suffering from the corrosion that can cost big bucks to put right, but I knew exactly what we needed to do with it. My plan was always to keep it absolutely original and just concentrate on a proper restoration, as I knew that was where the profit lay. I definitely had no intention of messing with this one. Retaining that originality was the only way to go.

long way to restoring the magic of the Jaguar's traditional cabin.

Next up was replacing the torn door card on the driver's side. It was a simple job to unscrew the fixtures, including the door handle, armrest and window winder handle. Normally a bit of care would have been taken in removing the old panel to prevent damage, but this one was ready for replacement so releasing the securing clips was a quick job. The new panel – sourced from a specialist – clipped easily into place, and with the fittings screwed back on it was another job ticked off the list. Fortunately the popularity of the E-Type means that a huge range of trim parts is available, and improving a tired interior makes a big difference – often it's a DIY task too, which can help to save money on a project. All that remained was for the old front footwell carpets to be replaced with new ones, and the freshly refurbished seats bolted back into place, and the cabin of the E-Type was looking great once more.

Job done

It had been lot of work for poor old Edd. Repairing the bodywork and replacing the exhaust system had taken time, but there was also the matter of a big extra job in the form of the leaking differential oil seal. The budget had taken a hammering too, with plenty of new parts required – never cheap on a car like this that deserved the best – but the E-Type was finally finished. All that work had added up to a hefty total, the Jaguar costing a final £16,090, so Mike would have to be at his sharpest to gain a healthy profit. That meant advertising the car on specialist websites with a price tag of £19,000 – the highest yet on *Wheeler Dealers*. But Mike's selling skills paid off once again. The new owner paid £18,500 for this evocative and stylish coupe, and the show had rescued one of the finest cars ever built.

Final test drive

After such a special project, Mike and Edd thoroughly deserved to experience the finished Jaguar, although perhaps icy country roads weren't the best environment for such a legendary sports car. Not to worry, though, as the E-Type coped perfectly with the tricky conditions, and with Mike enjoying every moment behind the wheel it was clear just how proud they both were. And thanks to that V12 engine and the new exhaust system it drove and sounded as good as it looked. Was it the pinnacle of *Wheeler Dealers* so far? Well, Mike certainly thought so.

Lamborghini Urraco S

Whenever the name Lamborghini is mentioned most people think of the futuristic Countach, with its sharply defined wedge shape and dramatic scissor doors. But there were plenty of other models too, including this, the Urraco. The work of talented designer Marcello Gandini, the name means 'little bull'. It was launched at the 1970 Turin Motor Show, but it would be almost three years before customers got their hands on this stylish coupé. With 2+2 seating and a transversely mounted 2.5-litre V8 engine, this was a rapid way to transport four people, and in 'S' specification there was a luxurious and stylish leather and suede-clad interior too.

With the time having arrived for *Wheeler Dealers* to get another Italian thoroughbred into the workshop Mike was determined to find one of these rare classics for Edd to work his magic on. But with fewer than 800 produced, tracking one down wasn't going to be easy, and it took plenty of searching and a trawl through Mike's contact book before one was found. The only problem was that the car was in Poland, so a long trip was needed if this particular deal was to be done. What he found was an early example – perhaps one of the first 25 made – with fantastic period green paintwork, and while it looked to be in good condition there were a few problems to contend with.

In fact this wasn't to be a normal viewing and test drive, because not only was the car wedged into its parking spot but it also hadn't moved for around six years, and driving it was out of the question. Nor could

Jobs to be tackled

As Mike explains elsewhere, it had been a huge struggle just extricating the car from its storage place, and it was just as hard to get it into the workshop, so things were all set to involve some serious effort if big profits were to be made. That ancient cambelt would need replacing, involving the complete removal of the sonorous V8. And Mike had also spotted a problem with the clutch pedal, so that would also need to be tackled. But it wasn't going to end there. The complex arrangement of carburettors would require tuning, and the brakes would need refurbishing. Edd had plenty of hard work ahead of him then...

Just getting the Urraco out from its resting place was a challenge, as Mike found out.

It wasn't much easier getting it into the workshop, and a few hours were spent wrestling with it.

Improving access to the V8 meant removing the engine cover, the hinges proving easy to unbolt.

There was plenty to remove before the engine could come out, starting with the air boxes.

Mike hear it run, as a loose cambelt made this too much of a risk. So he had to rely on his years of experience and a quick chat with Edd before doing the deal. The master mechanic was quick to give it the thumbs-up, though, and having heeded his advice Mike was ready to spend the €25,000 that would guarantee it a place in the *Wheeler Dealers* hall of fame. At £21,500 at the time, this was serious money for the boys, and the most expensive car yet to feature on the show. But the rewards would be worth it.

Removing the engine

The only way to change the cambelt was to remove the engine first, a job that wasn't for the faint-hearted on a car like this, and one that even Edd found a bit daunting – but he was ready to get stuck in. To improve access to the cramped engine bay, the first task was to remove the louvred engine compartment cover, a matter of undoing the mounting bolts and removing the hinge pins. With that done he set to work on all of the components that would need to be removed and disconnected before the engine could come out, starting by unscrewing the retaining knobs and removing the top of the air boxes.

With the boxes removed, the next step was to disconnect all of the electrical wiring to the engine, taking care to label the wires and make copious notes of what went where to help with refitting. Already it had become clear just what a major task the engine removal was going to be, such as tackling the huge number of pipes and hoses to be removed, including those for the cooling and fuel systems. With the car on the ramp Edd could loosen the appropriate jubilee clips from underneath and drain out the coolant... and

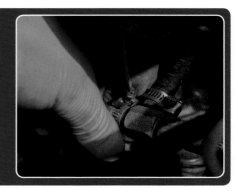

Lots of pipework to disconnect too, so Edd took notes to help with reassembly.

How much did it cost?

Car	£21,380
Shipping	£3,000
Clutch parts	£2,572
Belts and bearings	£208
Brakes	£76
Total	***£27,236***

it was at this stage that he spotted a problem that was likely to be responsible for the inoperative clutch: there was clutch fluid dripping from one of the hydraulic pipes.

The clutch issue would be tackled later. In the meantime there was still plenty to do to separate the engine from the car. The suspension would remain attached to the car, so the mounting points between subframe and body needed to be unbolted and the shock absorber lower mounts detached from the hubs. The work had taken plenty of hours so far – it wasn't a job to be rushed and definitely required a methodical approach – but things were progressing well, and it was time to undo the bolts that secured the subframe to the chassis. In the Urraco the engine and gearbox were mounted in the subframe, and with those bolts undone the whole lot could be lowered away from the car. It was done slowly, though, a stage at a time. A second pair of hands was useful here, to ensure that nothing became trapped between the subframe and the chassis, which would risk damaging delicate wiring and pipework or expensive engine ancillaries.

Such careful removal would also prevent damage if it turned out that Edd had forgotten to

disconnect anything, something that's easy to do when dealing with a car as complex as this one. He'd done a great job as always, however, and with the engine and gearbox removed it was on to the next stage.

Fixing the clutch

Separating the engine and gearbox

Before going much further it was clear that the engine and gearbox would need to be separated. The first step was to unbolt the exhaust system, including the rear silencer and the pipework up to the joints with the exhaust manifold on each side of the V8. As always, a bit of penetrating fluid would help loosen any stubborn nuts and bolts, but it all came apart easily enough and the exhaust itself was in good condition, which was great news for the budget.

The bolts securing the driveshafts to the gearbox were next, and with the hubs tilted back

A mirror can be a useful tool: Edd spotting the frayed clutch hose that was allowing hydraulic fluid to leak out.

With everything disconnected, the engine remained resting on a toolbox as the car was lifted up.

Engine removal

Removing a car's engine can seem a daunting task, but it's not as difficult as you might think. Here are some tips to help the job go smoothly:

- Before starting work make sure you have all the necessary tools. Consider buying or hiring an engine hoist and don't be afraid to ask for help.
- Buy a repair manual if one is available. It could save a lot of time and effort.
- Approach the job methodically and make a list of the tasks required. Don't just start by randomly removing parts.
- Give yourself as much access to the engine as possible, so consider removing items like the bonnet. It's usually a quick job and can make all the difference.
- Don't forget workshop safety! Disconnect the battery before starting work; drain engine fluids to make it lighter and prevent accidental spillages; have plenty of suitable material available in case of fuel, oil or coolant spills; and dispose of rags and waste safely.
- Have small bags or containers handy to store parts and fixings as they're removed, and label them accordingly. It can get very confusing otherwise. Label wires and hoses for the same reason.
- Don't rush the job, and remember to take notes or, better still, pictures to help with reassembly.

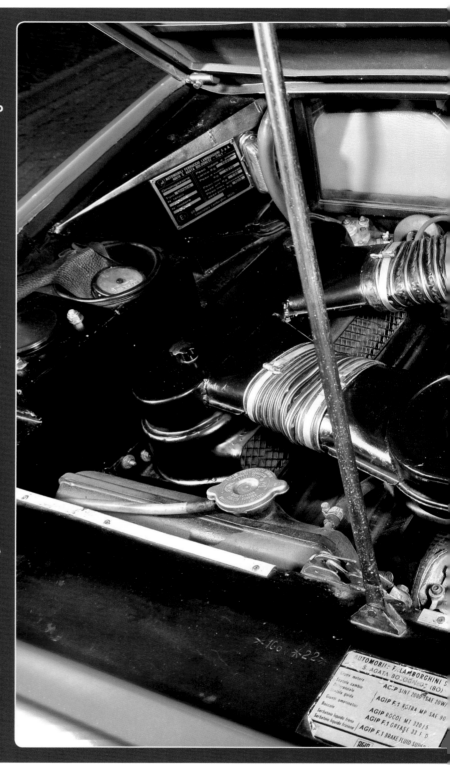

Edd got help separating the engine from its subframe before tackling the clutch problem.

With the exhaust and driveshafts removed, gentle persuasion helped separate the engine and gearbox.

Buying one

➜ **A complete restoration will swallow huge amounts of money, so every inch of the bodywork needs checking for damage or corrosion. Don't buy without an expert inspection.**

➜ **Any problems with the engine or gearbox are likely to be difficult and expensive to fix, and will likely need specialist attention. Watch for head gasket failure, oil leaks and worn fuel systems.**

➜ **Excessive noise from the gearbox or trouble selecting gears will need further investigation, and repairs are likely to be costly. Original Lamborghini parts are very pricey.**

➜ **Neither the suspension nor brakes are especially complex, but some parts are no longer available so ensure these systems haven't been neglected.**

➜ **Refurbishing a tired interior won't be cheap so avoid anything too decrepit, and ensure that all of the electrics are working as they should.**

for clearance the shafts were ready to be withdrawn (the hubs themselves would remain attached to the subframe.) Then, with the mounting bolts undone and the engine suspended from an engine crane using heavy-duty straps, the subframe was slid out of position. Next, with the bolts securing the engine to the transmission undone, a carefully applied pry bar helped to lever the two apart. Then it was time for a closer look at that clutch.

Clutch and hydraulic pipe replacement

Some investigation beneath the rear of the Lamborghini, using a small mirror to aid access, had revealed that the hydraulic pipe between the clutch master cylinder and slave cylinder had become chafed, hence the fluid leak. Removing the pipe was simple enough, as Edd just sawed through it at the slave cylinder connection – further damage wouldn't matter, as Mike would be sourcing a replacement. But undoing the four bolts and removing the cover plate for the clutch slave cylinder had revealed yet another problem: the return spring was missing. Most likely

Unbolting this access plate revealed another problem with the clutch – a broken return spring.

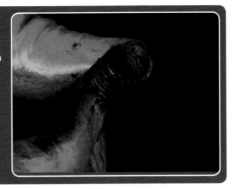

That broken clutch return spring, found at the bottom of the bell housing.

A special flywheel-locking tool prevents the engine from rotating once the cambelt is removed.

The clutch was in a poor state, with new parts costing a whopping £2,500.

The new clutch parts, along with the replacement hydraulic pipe that Mike had got made by a specialist.

it had snapped and the bits had fallen into the bellhousing, which as it turned out was exactly what had happened.

The first step in replacing the clutch was to lock the flywheel in place using a suitable tool to prevent it rotating, so that the clutch cover and pressure plate could be unbolted. With the cover removed it was clear that money would have to be spent – the friction plate was badly worn, and the surface of the pressure plate itself was pitted and corroded. Thankfully the friction plate could be refurbished with a new lining for just £37, but the rest had to be

bought new from Lamborghini at a cost of £2,500! With a new release bearing and slave cylinder also needed, the parts list was growing.

Sourcing a new pipe

Buying a new pipe as an original part from Lamborghini was going to cost over £100, so to keep the parts spend down Mike went to see a specialist who could make up a new pipe for a fraction of the price. With the old pipe as a guide the specialist was able to identify the connections and threads at each end – an unusual mix of 12mm

The bills were stacking up, so thankfully the new clutch spring was a cheap, easy fix.

It's a quick job to attach the new clutch pipe to the slave cylinder. No more leaks!

metric size at one end and imperial at the other. This wasn't a problem, though, and with the correct diameter of new braided hose selected and the new connectors crimped on, an adapter was the last bit required to finish the job. The new pipe had cost just £25, and Edd soon had it attached to the Urraco. With the new clutch fitted, and the new slave cylinder and return spring in place, it was job done, and with the engine out of the car it had taken just a couple of hours to complete.

Renewing the cambelt

Mike had already established that the cambelt was loose when he was in Poland, and there was no chance of starting the engine. But once it was back in the workshop Edd was able to explain that the Urraco's engine was of the 'interference' variety. That meant that if the belt snapped the pistons and valves would meet with expensive and destructive consequences, so replacing it was vital.

Preparation

First a bit of preparatory work was needed. The engine and gearbox were cleaned of oil and dirt to

make the job easier, and with the refrigerant gas safely removed from the air-conditioning system – it was important not to let the gas vent into the atmosphere – the pipework was disconnected and the air-conditioning pump was unbolted.

A few other pipes and hoses were also getting in the way, so these were removed along with the auxiliary drive belts; then the bolts securing the belt covers could be removed. Before going any further it was crucial to ensure that the valve timing marks were correctly aligned. Those on the camshaft pulleys were checked first, Edd using a strap wrench to rotate the crankshaft pulley. The mark for the crankshaft was actually on the flywheel and this could only be checked via an inspection window on the gearbox's bellhousing that carried corresponding marks. With the letters 'PMS' visible (the Italian equivalent of TDC, or 'top dead centre') he could be sure that the timing was spot-on. With the gearbox temporarily refitted to the engine Edd could identify TDC and then press on with the job.

Fitting the new belt

It was easy enough to release the tensioner pulley and remove the old belt but Edd also took the

Before tackling the cambelt Edd removes the air-conditioning compressor after safely discharging the system.

Before tackling the cambelt Edd made sure that the timing marks lined up.

opportunity to check the condition of the three idler pulleys. They looked OK on the surface but spinning them by hand revealed noisy bearings, and as the failure of those would be catastrophic for the engine he decided to replace them.

With the retaining bolts undone a puller tool was used to remove the pulleys; then a heavy-duty press was required to separate each pulley from its bearing. Some emery cloth and a dash of oil soon had the pulley surfaces looking as good

as new, and fortunately the bearings themselves were easy and relatively cheap to source. With the new bearings pressed into place and the securing circlips refitted, they were ready to go back on to the engine. The pulleys were located on their shafts with the help of a large socket, and securing circlips and bolts refitted.

Feeding on the new belt was an easy task. Then all that was needed was to rotate the engine by

There were various timing marks to check, and it's vital to get this right to avoid engine damage later.

One of the worn and noisy belt pulleys that Edd needed to replace.

With the securing bolt undone a puller was the best way to remove the pulleys.

A press is needed to remove and refit the pulley bearings. An engineering shop can help if you don't have one.

Handy tips

- Think about whether you can find a similar part from a different model, or, as with the clutch pipe, get a new part made up rather than buy an expensive original. It's not unusual for even exotic cars to share components with more run-of-the-mill models, and owners' clubs will know the best fixes for a particular model. It can save a lot of money during a restoration.
- Some jobs during a restoration – like the engine removal on the Lamborghini – can seem daunting at first, but it can be helpful to set yourself a deadline for completing the task. Mike and Edd always have a deadline to get the car finished and it definitely helps drive the project forward, and stops you from worrying about a task and putting it off.

hand for a couple of full revolutions just to ensure the timing marks were still aligned, and the job was finished. All that remained was to refit the belt covers and the pipework removed earlier, bolt the air-conditioning compressor back into place and refill the system with refrigerant gas. This last task was one that required suitable qualifications as well as specialist equipment, and while Edd luckily had both there are plenty of specialists who could do the job if necessary and at a reasonable cost. Edd's tip was never be tempted to tamper with an air-conditioning system yourself unless you have the necessary knowledge and tools – it's far safer to let an expert do it for you.

Finishing the engine work

With the new cambelt and clutch fitted things were progressing well with the Urraco's V8, but before it was reunited with the car Edd performed a minor service. Access was much easier with the engine on the bench, and it got a host of new parts, including spark plugs, HT leads and a new distributor cap. With the oil and air filters replaced, work could start on getting it back into the car.

The first job was to bolt it back into the subframe – which had had any surface corrosion removed and had received a fresh coat of paint while it was separated from the engine. But before that the gearbox was reattached to the engine and the exhaust system refitted. Once the engine was securely back in the subframe the driveshafts were bolted back to the transmission. And then the whole assembly was raised back into position beneath the car.

Again it was a case of doing this in several stages to ensure that it was correctly positioned, without causing damage to the bodywork or engine ancillaries. Then it was just a case of refitting all of the components, such as the suspension, cabling and pipework. As ever Edd took his time reconnecting everything, referring to the labels and notes he made earlier to make sure that nothing was forgotten. It was tempting to rush this aspect once all of the major work had been done, but a methodical approach now would save time sorting problems later. And of course, he was sure to top up all of the fluids such as the coolant before moving on to the next stage, firing up that impressive motor. A new battery was fitted first and the old fuel was drained from the tank and replaced with fresh unleaded along with some lead replacement additive (definitely a good point to remember with cars that might have been standing unused for long periods of time).

With the cambelt replaced, a minor service was carried out including a new distributor cap.

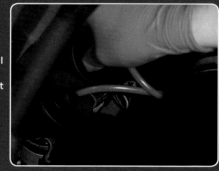

The coil connections are refitted before firing up that soulful V8. What a terrific noise it made too.

Though both Mike and Edd were eagerly anticipating this exciting moment, it was still important to exercise a bit of caution. With the engine having been removed, and of course not run for some years, it would have been unwise to just start it up. It was important to ensure that the oil had a chance to circulate around the engine first, so there would be proper lubrication of components when the engine was running. So with the twin ignition coils temporarily disconnected, the engine was turned over a few times to build up oil pressure. And then the moment of truth.

It was a bit of a tense moment in the workshop as the engine coughed and spluttered a few times – it would take time for those thirsty carburettors to fill up with fuel. But of course, they needn't have worried. Edd's expert fettling meant the glorious V8 finally fired into life and ran almost perfectly. The project was well on track, but before the Urraco could get back on the road there were a few other important jobs to tackle.

Tuning the carburettors

While it might not have had fuel injection, the fuel system fitted to the Lamborghini was still pretty complex, involving four twin-choke, downdraught carburettors. With effectively one choke per cylinder, getting them properly set up for maximum performance and efficiency was a tricky task that took skill and years of experience, so Edd employed the services of an expert, Tim, to get the job done. And as someone used to looking after the cars of a well-known collector, he was just the man for the job.

Access to the carburettors was needed, so the air boxes and inlet trumpets were removed first. But before the engine was started Edd ensured that extractor pipes were attached to the exhaust

Finding one of these cars for sale wasn't easy – there were hardly any around – but I knew as soon as I saw this Urraco that we'd found a great car. However, even with the deal done getting it out of storage was an absolute nightmare. It was pretty much rooted to the spot, and while moving it might have looked difficult on the show, in reality it was a lot worse! It was parked so close to the wall that I was worried about damaging the paintwork on that side of the car, and the whole thing took a good few hours in sub-zero temperatures to get the car into the trailer. And even then we still had to get it into the workshop. But once we got it there it was a great feeling to know we had an Italian supercar on the show. Even better was the test drive at the end, an absolutely epic experience and one that neither of us will ever forget.

so that the workshop wasn't filled with noxious fumes! It was important to ensure the ignition timing was spot-on before making any fuelling adjustments, consequently this was checked next using a proprietary timing gun, although thanks to the awkward positioning of the timing marks beneath the car this would need to be a two-man job. The timing needed to be set to 18° of advance, so with Tim checking the timing marks Edd loosened the clamp bolt and rotated the

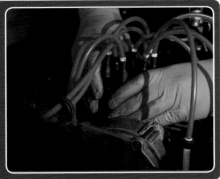

Before setting up the carburettors the ignition timing needs to be spot on, which means moving the distributor.

The timing is now perfect so it's time for the specialist to work his magic on those carbs.

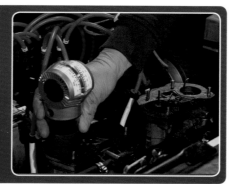
First job is checking the airflow, using this special meter placed on each carburettor choke.

Adjustments are made to the idle screw to balance the airflow between the cylinder banks.

Tweaking the air bleed screws ensured the suction through each choke was correct...

...and then just minor adjustments to the fuel/air mixture were required to get the engine running perfectly.

distributor until exactly the right measurement was reached. If other obstructions prevent the required rotation of the distributor, his handy tip is to remove the unit completely and refit it in a slightly different position before continuing with the timing adjustment.

With the distributor clamped firmly in position, it was on to the carburettors. The first job was to use a special meter on the chokes to check the airflow into each bank of cylinders. It was important that this was balanced correctly between the front and rear banks, and with the front bank (nearest the rear of the car) being slightly low, the idle screws were adjusted to get the balance just right.

The next task was checking and adjusting the amount of suction through each choke. This was altered by loosening the lock nut and tweaking the air bleed screws. It was a time-consuming task, with myriad adjustments and rechecking required, but an important one nonetheless if the engine was to perform at its best. With the job almost finished, Tim used his expert ear to adjust the fuel and air mixture for each carburettor, making small adjustments to the idle mixture screw to ensure it was perfect. The engine was running beautifully and sounded wonderful, and with Edd reckoning that the job would have cost around £500 at a Lamborghini specialist some money had been saved too. Now it was time to tackle the brakes.

Refurbishing the brakes

With this sort of performance on offer – the vivid green Lambo could hit 60mph in less than seven seconds and reach almost 150mph – it was pretty important to make sure the Urraco stopped as well as it went, so plenty of time was spent checking and refurbishing the braking system. The brakes had been locked solid when Mike inspected the car but it appeared that the vibration during transit had freed them almost completely, which certainly made the job easier.

Firstly the condition of the brake lines was checked, and with their integrity meeting Edd's high standards the discs were cleaned with a water-based solvent and dried using an airline. Fortunately their overall condition was fine, apart from some surface corrosion, especially where they had been stuck to the pads – which was just

New brake discs weren't available, so Edd got to work cleaning up the old ones. Luckily they were still serviceable.

A handy tool helps check the amount of pad material left.

New brake pads were cheap – just £70 – and they were easy to fit too.

as well, as new ones weren't available – but they needed a more thorough clean. The brake calipers were unbolted, and with the discs accessible the lip around the edge was ground back using a light grinding disc, and the surface cleaned using a wire brush attachment on the grinder.

The brake calipers were also in good condition, and with those cleaned it was time for a new set of pads. Although measurement showed there was still plenty of friction material left on them they were somewhat old, so definitely worth replacing. With the retaining pins carefully tapped out the old pads were withdrawn from the calipers, and with a new set costing just £70 this was a cheap fix. Copper grease was applied to the pad mounting points and backplates before refitting them into the caliper, and once the retaining pins had been securely refitted the brakes were almost done.

All that was needed to complete the job was a full refill with fresh brake fluid and the system bled to purge any trapped air, Edd advising viewers to check that the bleed nipples are securely tightened after such work to prevent brake failure!

Job done

Wheeler Dealers had had a true supercar in the workshop, and while Mike had taken a risk buying an Italian thoroughbred that he hadn't even heard running, let alone driven, the gamble had paid off. Not only did the finished Lamborghini Urraco look fantastic, it was also in superb mechanical health thanks to Edd's skill and dedication. The car was advertised for sale at £37,500, and, after a superb trip to a Lamborghini gathering in Italy, Mike managed to sell the Urraco for a whopping £35,000. Big money for a big project, but as usual the boys had pulled it off in style.

Final test drive

Such a special project deserved a special test drive, and that's exactly what happened as the boys headed to Italy to take part in the 50th anniversary celebrations of the marque. In Bologna they'd be joining the biggest parade of Lamborghinis in the world, with 350 cars taking part. They'd be surrounded by Miuras to Murcielagos and everything in between. And it was Edd's turn to get behind the wheel. It was a great birthday treat, and he was clearly enjoying himself winding through the snow-capped mountains. The stunning coupe looking right at home on the sinuous roads, and as they negotiated the tight hairpin bends Mike had visions of *The Italian Job* with its wonderful Matt Monroe soundtrack. And the Urraco performed superbly, accompanied by the noise from that wonderful V8 engine echoing off the mountains.

They had to sneak into the piazza – against official orders – to join the other gathered cars, but it was worth it, although unfortunately the trip wasn't entirely plain sailing. A seized brake caliper presented an unexpected mechanical problem and one that needed fixing before the rest of the trip

Both of us really had to push to get the Lamborghini on the show, but it was something we really wanted to do, especially with the 50th anniversary of the marque. With models like the Countach far too expensive we settled on the Urraco, as it was much cheaper and still a really pretty car. The one we found in Poland was pretty much ideal – the factory colour was very cool, and once we were able to get it started it sound pretty awesome too!

Working on it was wasn't as bad as I thought it might be – it was fiddly rather than especially difficult, but the same can be said for a lot of older Italian cars. The Lancia Integrale we did on the show once was the same. A few of the jobs weren't that straightforward but for me it was still a real joy to work on, and I would have loved to buy it myself.

could be enjoyed. And unfortunately that wasn't the only unexpected issue they encountered, the other involving the tuning of the carburettors. Having had these tuned in the UK, Mike and Edd discovered that the engine of the Urraco was really struggling to cope in the high altitudes of the Italian mountains. The thin air was playing havoc with the V8, sapping power and causing the engine to run poorly, so some further hasty retuning was necessary – not an especially easy job given the need to remove parts of the induction system for access; and it required yet more adjustment once back at a lower altitude. But it was all part of the challenge of this exciting Italian classic, and certainly wasn't going to spoil their enjoyment of a fantastic test drive.

Fit for the Road

Land Rover Discovery

Back in the late 1980s Land Rover needed a model that would bridge the gap between the agricultural but capable Defender and the luxurious Range Rover. That model was the Discovery, which arrived in 1989 to much acclaim from the motoring press. It was still based on a sturdy separate chassis, but the smart styling with its 'Alpine light' windows looked as at home on the school run as it did crossing a mountain range, and the 'Disco' retained all of the company's legendary off-road capability. And those looks were matched by a robust but stylish interior that was the work of noted designers Conran Design, headed by Terence Conran.

With credentials like these it was no wonder Mike wanted to get his hands on one, but instead of using the Internet he opted for the old-fashioned search method. Heading to a local cafe and grabbing a mug of tea, he scoured the classified magazine ads in search of a bargain. He'd already discounted the V8 petrol model as being too thirsty, so his search focused on the tough diesel engine, and he soon found one that looked perfect for the job. The 1995 2.5-litre TDi turbodiesel had covered a hefty 150,000 miles, but it looked good, had the desirable manual gearbox, and the owner wanted just £1,700. It was time to pay them a visit and apply those *Wheeler Dealers* skills.

His first job was to give it a thorough check over, looking

Jobs to be tackled

The Discovery was in pretty good shape, but there was a problem with the steering that would need fixing, and Mike had plans for this particular project. Already capable off-road, the boys were going to turn the Disco into an even more serious mud-plugger that would be able to tackle any terrain. That meant a few modifications were called for, including the fitting of some protective parts, upgrades to the lighting, and the fitting of a snorkel that would improve the car's wading capabilities. With a challenging test drive planned for the end of the project, Edd certainly had his work cut out with this one.

for any signs of oil leaks or underbody damage caused by clumsy off-roading. But it looked promising, as this particular example was in good condition. The test drive went quite well too, even if performance was somewhat pedestrian, but the big off-roader had plenty of charm and Mike was certain that this was the car he wanted. It wasn't perfect though, as he identified a steering system that felt very vague – even for a 4x4 on chunky tyres – so that would be a job for Edd to sort. He also had a plan for this particular Discovery, which was to improve its off-road credentials and turn it into an expedition vehicle by fitting a few well-chosen extras. After a bit of expert haggling the car was his for just £1,500, and the project could get under way.

Fixing the steering

Assessing the problem

The vague feel to the steering that Mike had complained of could have had a number of causes, so Edd's first job was to examine the 'Disco' to try to identify the problem, starting with the tyre pressures. As he explained, the high profile construction of off-road tyres could make such cars prone to less accurate steering, the taller rubber moving around more as the car went down the road, but tyres that weren't correctly inflated could easily exaggerate the problem. The pressures on this car were all OK, though, at around 26psi, so further investigation was going to be needed.

With the 'Disco' up on the ramp (if you don't

have one available, Edd advises making sure you use suitably heavy-duty axle stands, as 4x4s are heavy vehicles), he could take a closer look at all of the steering and suspension components to see if anything was amiss, and with Paul inside the car turning the steering wheel from lock to lock Edd hoped to spot excess play in any of the various balljoints. With problems like these it is always best to take a methodical approach to the diagnosis and try to eliminate possible causes as you go along, so that's exactly what he did, examining each joint in turn looking for signs of wear or excessive movement.

Discovering they were all fine, the next check was the power steering damper, but this didn't reveal any leaks either. Instead, it soon became clear that the steering box itself was the culprit, with too much slack visible as the wheels were turned. Adjustment wasn't possible in this case, so a replacement unit was the only answer.

Fitting the new steering box

A brand new part would have left a big hole in the budget, so Edd opted to fit a reconditioned box instead, which cost just £160. As he explained it was often preferable to choose a reconditioned rather than a pattern part. That way you'd be getting a good quality original item that had just been refurbished, rather than a copy where the materials and tolerances might not be as good. Of course, there are very good pattern parts available, but it was an excellent tip as always and one to remember when planning the budget for a restoration.

With the new part having arrived there was plenty of work to do as always before it could be fitted, and the first step was to disconnect the hydraulic pipes from the top of the steering box. These unscrewed easily using a crow's-foot spanner,

How much did it cost?

Car	£1,500
Steering box	£167
Underbody protection	£130
Roof rack and ladder	£500
Spotlights and light grilles	£190
Snorkel	£244
Total	*£2,731*

but Edd was careful to avoid too much fluid escaping and leaving a mess on the workshop floor.

The universal joint between the steering column and the steering box was the next item to be unbolted, leaving Edd to concentrate on disconnecting the track rod ends from the wheel hub. With the securing bolts undone it was just a matter of breaking the tapers using two hammers, tapping them from each side of the joint (though you could always use a ball-joint splitter tool to do the job instead). As Edd would tell you, the heavier duty components used in 4x4s can make such jobs tougher than on other cars, so it's important to have the right tools available, and a big pry bar is always handy to help separate any joints. Bear in mind too that on an older example, or one that's seen plenty of action in the mud, the securing bolts for suspension and steering parts could be corroded so applying plenty of penetrating fluid before you start work is always a good idea. You might also need to apply

The vague steering Mike had complained of was a worry, but all the ball joints looked OK.

The arm from the steering box didn't look worn either, so the problem clearly lay with the box itself.

Edd struggles with the heavy steering box, a reconditioned item keeping the parts spend down.

The new steering box bolts back in but wheel alignment will need checking after a job like this.

Bleeding the air from the steering hydraulics is the last step, and the steering system is fixed.

Edd carefully marks the front bumper prior to cutting away the lower section.

some heat to seized fixings so Edd was prepared to break out the oxy-acetylene torch, but he was lucky in this case as everything came apart fairly easily.

With everything disconnected, the last step was unbolting the steering box from its mounting point on the chassis and manoeuvring it out from beneath the car – not an easy job, as the unit was both awkward and heavy. Not that it would defeat this master mechanic, who soon had the reconditioned part bolted back into position and could start on reconnecting the track-rod ends and steering-column joint – making sure, of course, that everything was done up to the correct torque, vital when you're dealing with steering components. Also worth noting was that the new unit came with dust covers protecting the hydraulic pipe connections, and to prevent dirt ingress these would only be removed at the last minute.

When working on the steering, the brakes or the fuel system it is always worth taking the time to clean any dirt and debris from around pipe connections and components before disconnecting them, and to consider using suitable bungs to prevent contaminants getting in. Anyhow, with the hydraulic pipes reconnected at the steering box and the system replenished with fresh fluid, bleeding the system of air was a simple matter of starting the engine and turning the steering wheel from lock to lock. That way any air bubbles would be expelled through the fluid reservoir – the steering should feel nice and smooth once this has happened, with no notchiness as it's turned. The system then just needed a final top up. The steering was sorted, and it was time for some exciting modifications.

The off-road modifications

Protecting the bodywork and mechanicals

If the Discovery was going to be ready to tackle any terrain – and there was a rather special road test planned – some major changes were going to be needed, starting with the front bumper. The plastic air dam beneath the bumper would be easily damaged during serious off-roading, so Edd got to work removing it. The centre section was attached to the metal bumper and to the two corner sections and was easily removed, but the section of air dam at each corner would need to be cut away. He started by marking the section to be removed using masking tape, and once happy with the

The differential protector simply bolts on, so a nice easy job for Edd.

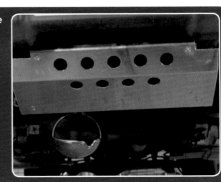

The skid plate is another bolt-on part and will provide vital protection in the rough stuff.

measurements a cutting disc was used to separate it from the main corner section. With any rough edges carefully smoothed away he could move on to protecting the exposed mechanical parts.

A heavy-duty differential protector was purchased and it took just minutes to fit. With the unit located around the front of the differential, the clamp at the top was firmly tightened and it was job done. Another was attached to the rear differential in the same way. Next up was a skid plate that would protect the bottom of the engine from damage, and it was another item that was easy to fit. Mounting brackets were bolted to the chassis, and with those firmly secured the plate itself was bolted into position. With all of that done Mike and Edd could be sure that exposed mechanical parts wouldn't be damaged.

Fitting a roof rack and ladder

The 'Disco' needed to be capable of taking on any expedition, so extra carrying capacity would come in handy, and that meant the addition of a roof rack. Once again this would prove an easy job for Edd, the rack just mounting to the roof guttering – although an extra pair of hands was useful in fitting the unwieldy item into position. There were eight mounting points in all, and with the clamps located beneath the gutters they could be secured with the washers and nuts included in the kit.

But a way of accessing the extra storage would be needed, and that came in the form of a ladder mounted at the rear of the Landie. This would prove to be a slightly more fiddly job, and one that needed a careful and methodical approach to ensure it would be safe and secure.

The first task was to unscrew the rear number plate, as the base of the ladder would be mounted just below the tailgate's handle and lock. As always

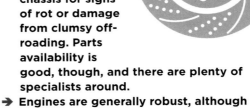

Buying one

➜ Check for panel damage and inspect the chassis for signs of rot or damage from clumsy off-roading. Parts availability is good, though, and there are plenty of specialists around.

➜ Engines are generally robust, although lack of regular maintenance can be an issue. Watch for coolant and oil leaks, while TDi diesels can suffer from cracked cylinder heads.

➜ The thirsty V8 petrol engine is probably best avoided, but if you're tempted watch for signs of overheating that could have blown the head gaskets, and for rough running.

➜ Excessive noise from the four-wheel-drive system spells trouble. And check for oil leaks from the transfer box and differentials. Regular towing puts a strain on gearboxes too.

➜ Interiors can take a battering, so check for trim damage and ensure all the gadgets are working. Leaking sunroofs can be an issue.

The roof rack is easy to bolt on, just affixing to the roof gutters.

Fixing brackets come as part of the kit. It's important to make sure they're securely tightened.

Marking the tailgate before holes are drilled for the lower ladder mounting. Remember: measure twice, cut once!

These clever 'riv-nuts' are secured into the skin of the tailgate ready for the mounting points to screw in.

it was a case of 'measure twice and cut once', so before drilling the mounting holes Edd carefully measured the correct location and applied masking tape to prevent the drill bit from slipping. Using a high speed steel (HSS) drill bit, two small pilot holes were drilled first before the correct-sized drill bit was used to enlarge them for the ladder mountings.

As the rear of the tailgate panel was inaccessible – meaning there would be no chance of using a conventional nut and bolt to secure the ladder – Edd chose to use clever fixings called 'riv-nuts'. Essentially these are part rivet and part threaded nut, and were fitted using a hand-held tool that resembles a rivet gun and inserts a threaded fixing into the panel skin ready to accept the bolt. The same method was used to insert fixings at the top of the tailgate channel, as the top the ladder fitted over the top edge of the tailgate. And with the ladder mounted and the bolts tightened, all that remained was for the number plate to be screwed back on and it was another job completed. A quick test of the new roof rack – involving Paul and some time-lapse filming – showed just how useful the extra storage capacity could be, although the test would prove more than a little exhausting for Edd's assistant!

Fitting the spotlights

No proper expedition vehicle would be complete without extra lighting to guide the driver through any challenges, so Mike splashed out over £150 for a smart pair of spotlights that would adorn the Discovery's front bumper. A bit of thought was needed before fitting, though, Edd considering a number of factors including whether to wire the spotlights so they illuminated with the headlamps on full beam or via a separate switch (he chose the former); thinking about the accessibility of the fuse and relay that would be needed, and making sure they were located out of

reach of any water ingress; ensuring the wiring was of the correct specification to deal with the electrical power required; and considering whether the alternator would cope with the extra load. Edd's tip is always to consider this last aspect before making any major electrical modifications, as there is often scope to fit an uprated part. It wasn't necessary in this case, though, and he could get straight on with fitting the new lights.

They would be mounted on a separate stainless steel bar attached to the front bumper, so fitting that was the first stage. Edd started by unbolting the plastic section of the bumper that contained the number plate and overriders, and with the metal section revealed he could get on with marking the position for the mounting bar. With the marks made and masking tape applied to prevent the drill slipping, pilot holes were made first before being enlarged with the correct size of drill bit. The plastic section of bumper removed previously was also measured, marked with tape and drilled, and with that replaced the mounting bar could be securely bolted into position. As he pointed out, not only did it look smart but it was also more pedestrian-friendly than the old-fashioned bull bars.

With the spotlights trial-fitted to the mounting

With the bumper measured and marked, the mounting holes for the light bar are drilled.

The plastic section of the bumper also needs drilling. Making a smaller pilot hole first is often easier.

It's best to test fit the lights early on so that any problems can be rectified before they are permanently attached.

Edd is checking the headlamp wiring connector to identify the high-beam terminal.

The relay acts as a switch and will turn on the spotlights when the headlamp high beam is selected.

bar to confirm the positioning, he was happy and could get on with the job of wiring them in. This could be done without disconnecting the battery, making it easier to identify the relevant connections; but as he explained, it wouldn't be a problem if you preferred to carry out electrical work with it disconnected. A main earth wire would be secured to the mounting bar itself, but more important was identifying the high beam terminal in the headlight's multi-plug connector – that way the spotlights would only come on when the headlights were on full beam, giving maximum illumination off-road.

With the headlights switched on a multimeter was used to identify the correct terminal, and with that done fitting the relay was next. This would trigger the spotlights when the high beam was activated, and some of Edd's wiring skills were needed. Via a fuse for extra protection, the wire carrying power to the relay was run from the battery, with the earth wire secured beneath the relay's mounting screw. The relay then needed to be connected to the headlamp wiring, so he used a suitable wire-stripping tool to expose a section of the high-beam wire and soldered in a new wire that would go to the low current side of the relay.

The relay is neatly mounted on the inner wing, with an earth wire secured below the mounting screw.

Tapping into the feed for the headlamp high beam means stripping back the insulation.

No bodged wiring here. Edd solders the wire in place for a reliable connection.

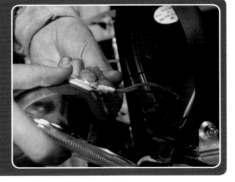

Connecting the wiring at the lamps is the last job. Upgrading lights is a DIY task and worth doing.

Land Rover Discovery timeline

1989 Project Jay officially becomes the Discovery. In three-door form only (to protect Range Rover sales), there are 2.5-litre turbodiesel and 3.5-litre V8 petrol engines, and plenty of Rover Group parts including Austin Allegro door handles! A five-door bodyshell and fuel injection for the V8 arrived in 1990.

1993 The fleet-friendly 2.0-litre MPi petrol engine seemed a good way of expanding sales, but poor performance and even poorer sales saw it quietly dropped not long after.

1994 The first major facelift, bringing a new 300TDi diesel engine and a 3.9-litre version of the V8. Looking similar to the original, main changes were limited to revised head and tail lights and interior tweaks.

1998 The Discovery 2 arrives, and this time there are major changes, including a 4.0-litre V8 and a larger body. It looked similar, but few panels were carried over.

2004 The Discovery 3 introduces a smoother new look, revised engines and a luxury interior. The use of air suspension is new too.

2009 Further cosmetic changes and a revised engine range mark out the Discovery 4. The cabin is more luxurious than ever but it retains the legendary off-road ability.

2014 Over a million examples have been sold and a new model, the Discovery Sport, is announced to replace the Freelander range.

Riv-nuts and adhesive were used to secure these protective rear light grilles.

The front light grilles just screw into place.

With the new joint protected by electrical tape, the final stage was to connect the high current side of the relay to the spotlights, and once the units were securely bolted to the mounting bar the Land Rover's lighting modifications were almost complete. All that was left was to ensure the wiring inside the spotlights was securely connected, then the lenses could be clipped and screwed to the body of the lamps. A quick test in a darkened workshop revealed that the Disco now had all the lighting power needed to tackle night-time manoeuvres. The last job was to fit some protective grilles over the light units. These just screwed on at the front, while at the rear they were stuck on at the outer edge and secured on the inner edge by more of those handy 'riv-nuts'.

Attaching a snorkel

There is a huge range of parts available if you want to improve the looks or ability of your off-roader, and the popularity of the Discovery mean's it's served better than most when it comes to making upgrades. And this would be the last job for the project.

There is nothing more ruinous for an engine than allowing water to enter the air intake. Once the cylinders have filled with liquid the result is usually terminal damage to the major components, and the chances are you'd need a whole new engine. Serious off-roading can involve wading through deep water, so a car like the Discovery is at more risk of damage, but there is an answer: fit a snorkel that allows the air intake to be mounted

◀ This particular example is a bit more extreme, but the skid plates, extra spotlights. and differential protector are all present and correct. The boys were obviously spot-on with the project car then.

much higher up, out of harm's way. This *Wheeler Dealers* car was going to be all about serious off-road capability, so Mike delved into the budget and spent almost £300 on a special kit, making sure he bought a good quality item as this would make fitting a lot easier for the hard-worked mechanic. Over to Edd, then.

The first job was going to need the most care – drilling the holes in the nearside wing. It was vital to get these just right, as a mistake at that stage could result in a new wing being needed. The snorkel kit came with a template, which was fitted over the body of the snorkel to ensure that all of the mounting points aligned correctly, and holes were marked to avoid any mistakes. With that done, Edd temporarily fixed the template to the wing with the sort of light adhesive used to mount pictures in frames (a handy tip as always, as the glue won't damage bodywork and can also be used to temporarily hold other components, such as brackets, in place). The position of the seven mounting holes, and main air inlet hole, could then be carefully marked on the wing itself, Edd taking his time and rechecking the measurements to get it just right.

Some further preparation was required before

Getting this wrong would be a disaster, so Edd takes his time positioning the snorkel template.

Once happy with the measurements, pilot holes are drilled for the snorkel mounting on the wing.

A large cutter attachment was needed to drill the main air intake hole. Edd needed a steady hand!

The mounting holes were finished using a step-drill that ensured they were exactly the right depth.

The thing I remember about the Discovery was that it was really about the first time we started to tailor the content of the show around the test drive we'd be taking at the end. Mostly we'd just drive the finished car somewhere scenic, but for the Land Rover we'd already decided that we were going to put it through its paces on an off-road course, so basically the finished car had to be capable of doing the job. We were using Land Rover's own test course, so the last thing we wanted was to embarrass ourselves in front of all their experts with a car that got stuck somewhere. So we decided right from the off that whatever we did with it had to turn it into a properly capable off-roader, and I think we achieved that.

any drilling took place. Working under the bonnet, Edd removed the air filter element and then set about disconnecting the original intake trunking; then the air filter housing itself could be removed. Further access would be needed, so with the securing screws undone the plastic wheel-arch liner was removed. Then it was on to the trickiest part of the job. Pilot holes were drilled first for the snorkel mountings, which were enlarged to the correct 16mm size using a step drill to ensure they were also of the correct depth. The drill bit had specific stages for different depths, so it was marked with some tape to avoid any mistakes. The main air inlet hole was made using a cutter attachment on the drill. This careful approach had paid off, though, and with the holes done perfectly it was just a case of de-burring the edges and applying a dab of paint to the exposed metal to prevent future corrosion.

The wing-mounted section could now be secured in place from inside the wheel arch, although Edd does admit that it was a fiddly task with plenty of potential to drop the various fixings as they were attached. Using a magnetic toolkit was a handy way of ensuring nothing vital went missing.

The next stage involved some modifications to the original air-filter housing. The first task was fitting a cap that would block off the original air inlet. Then the plastic fins on the side of the housing were ground away so that the new inlet hole could be drilled and the inlet flange fitted. A bead of sealant was applied first, and with the flange secured with three rivets more sealant was applied to ensure it was completely watertight. The original mounting lugs were cut off, as the housing would be fitted with an adaptor plate that would position it slightly differently in the engine bay once the snorkel was in place.

With the drain holes in the bottom of the housing plugged – there would be no point in

The new inlet flange was riveted to the air filter housing, a smear of sealant keeping things watertight.

Edd offers up the snorkel to the front wing. Luckily all the mounting holes were perfect.

Fitting the snorkel inlet was the final step, and the Disco was ready to tackle deep water.

allowing water to enter that way – the housing was bolted back into position, the trunking fed through the wing, and the external snorkel connected. All that was left was to attach the air inlet to the top of the snorkel using a jubilee clip, and the Discovery would be safe to enter deep water without fear of expensive damage.

Job done

Fitting the snorkel marked the end of this particular project, which had involved plenty of hours for Edd to turn the tough Landie into a perfect expedition vehicle. It looked fantastic and was ready for anything, but unfortunately it wasn't a car that was going to earn the boys big money. Mike advertised the Discovery for £3,400, but it was a tough market out

▼ Just like the *Wheeler Dealers* project, this one has the snorkel fitted, which massively improves the wading ability in deep water.

there, and it finally sold for just £3,000. With a total spend of £2,700 the profits were small, but it didn't matter, as they had turned this run-of-the-mill off-roader into something far more exciting and capable.

Final test drive

As Mike explains elsewhere, they were both quite nervous about taking the Discovery to Land Rover's test track, but they needn't have worried. The off-road modifications had paid off, and with Edd taking the wheel the Disco coped with every obstacle the course could throw at it. From clambering up steep and slippery gradients to wading axle-deep through muddy water, there was nothing it couldn't manage. It was the perfect finale to this tricky project, and a great demonstration of how a few careful upgrades and modifications can add real ability to a car. Plus plenty of hours in the workshop of course!

Working on a Discovery isn't actually too difficult. They are pretty rugged cars, access to components is fairly straightforward and everything fits together logically.

The one thing I did find, though, is that the hefty engineering means you need proper tools that can cope with the heavy-duty fixings; and some of the parts themselves – like that steering box – are seriously heavy, so it's worth thinking about health and safety before tackling one of these. An extra pair of hands is definitely useful, and to be honest I'd say that's a good thing anyway when you're working on a restoration project. There's no point in struggling alone, it's more fun and safer to have some help, and camaraderie is what the classic car scene is all about.

But going back to the Discovery, the other thing I'd say is that if it's seen a bit of off-road use, it's definitely worth giving the underside a thorough clean before tackling some jobs. If it's covered in mud the last thing you want is dirt entering delicate components, so a bit of preparation will make the job easier.

Mazda MX-5

With the demise of affordable two-seat roadsters there was clearly a gap in the market, and it was one that Mazda was about to fill in spectacular style. Taking inspiration from classics like the MGB and Lotus Elan, 1989 saw the introduction of the little MX-5, and it proved a hit with buyers from the moment it went on sale. The recipe was almost perfect, blending a lightweight body with a punchy twin-cam engine, a rifle-bolt gearchange and a simple but comfortable cabin. With just enough power to have fun, it handled beautifully, and a future classic had been born.

It was no surprise, then, that Mike would want to get his hands on one, and a chilly February day – the perfect time to buy a convertible, as prices are generally lower in the winter, rather than in the summer when everyone is after a drop-top – found him searching the classifieds where he'd find plenty of MX-5s for sale. One particular car caught his eye, though, a G-plate example on offer for just £1,750; so he headed straight for a viewing.

The car was honest and original, and the fun test drive sold it to him, but the little Mazda wasn't without a few issues. There were signs of corrosion, a scruffy convertible roof, and a particularly smelly cabin! In fact the extent of the interior problems would be greater than they thought, the damage to the roof and interior trim being far worse than it first appeared; but Mike had no choice but to grab this bargain convertible and rely on Edd to get the problems sorted. Still, such issues weren't going to put off the famous wheeler dealer – he knew it was the perfect car for Edd to work his magic on, and after a bit of haggling the car was his for £1,600.

Jobs to be tackled

There was plenty of work to do on the little roadster, so it looked like Edd would be burning the midnight oil on this one (Mike too, as it turned out, thanks to that awful interior). A new roof would be needed to replace the torn and tattered original, and there was the matter of renovating that smelly cabin. The biggest job, though, would be sorting the corrosion that had left a nasty hole in the windscreen pillar, and once Edd had put his body repair skills to the test he could turn his attention to adding some performance upgrades to the engine and suspension that would ensure the Mazda drove and handled as well as it looked. With lots of work to do, it was time to get started.

Before removing that nasty hood the seat belt mountings had to be unbolted.

The tatty hood was finally out but there was plenty more work before a new one could be fitted.

There were lots of screws to undo to remove the old hood cover, a job that needed plenty of patience.

Drilling out the hood rivets needed care to avoid damaging the frame itself.

Replacing the roof

Preparation

With a socket set and screwdrivers being all that was needed, Edd set to work removing the old hood and frame. Access would be needed to the frame mountings, so the first parts to be removed were the side trim panels (attached by various clips and screws), which was done carefully to prevent any damage, as these parts would be refitted later. The upper seat belt mountings were next – these just unbolted – and then Edd squeezed himself into the cosy interior with the hood raised to enable access to the screws that secured the rear of the hood cover itself.

Once all these jobs had been done the hood frame could be unbolted at each side of the car and the whole lot removed, taking care not to damage any interior trim or paintwork as it was withdrawn. With it out of the car it was a simple job to unbolt the hinges from the frame so that the hood cover itself could be tackled later in the project.

Fitting the new hood

This was a job that was going to test Edd's patience to the limit, and while tackling it himself would save substantial labour costs this fiddly and awkward job needed a lot of care for a perfect finish. As he himself admitted, although it is a task you could have a go at yourself even professional trimmers would take a few hours to get it done, so it paid to be ready for some hard work.

With the easily-damaged rear screen protected – masking paper or heavy-duty plastic was ideal – the first job was to separate the damaged hood cover from the frame, a task that involved undoing the numerous screws and clips that held everything together. As always these were carefully stored, as they'd be needed later, and it paid to take pictures or notes of where everything went. There were also plenty of rivets to drill out – carefully, though, to avoid damaging the frame.

With the two parts separated it was time to fit the new hood, Edd starting by attaching it to the frame at the centre seam, which when finished would be hidden by a section of trim. Reattaching the cover to the front and rear of the frame meant refitting all of those screws and clips and using a rivet gun to insert new rivets at various points. But the hardest part of the job was getting the correct tension in the hood. It was vital to get it right at this stage; if the tension was wrong, as it was permanently

With the rivets and screws refitted the MX-5 had a fresh new hood, and one that was weatherproof!

How much did it cost?

Car	£1,600
Seats and carpets	£135
Windscreen	£150
Performance air filter	£65
Wheels and tyres	£300
Interior and exterior trim	£270
Hood	£195
Total	**£2,715**

attached to the frame, the hood would sag when it was raised – not the look Mike or Edd were hoping for. So some brute force was required to stretch the material over the frame to get that tension just right. Cold temperatures in the workshop didn't help and it would have been helpful to apply some heat to the material if possible, making the roof more pliable and far easier to fit. The effort had paid off, though, and with the hood and frame complete the hinges were reattached and the whole arrangement was then bolted back into the car.

All that was left was to refit the screws at the base of the hood, refit the seat-belt mountings (ensuring the mounting bolts were done up to the correct torque on this vital bit of safety equipment) and refit the side trim panels in the cabin. The torn and leaky old hood was gone and the MX-5 was well on the way to becoming a smart little roadster again.

▼ No, not a new assistant for Edd, but an owner demonstrating how easy the hood was to use.

History of the MX-5

Ex-motoring journalist Rob Hall is widely credited with suggesting the MX-5 back in 1979, but it was 1984 before designers – including Shigenori Fukuda, Tsutomu 'Tom' Matano and Mark Jordan – started work. With the involvement of senior designer Shunji Tanaka, development work by British studio IAD and an impressive demonstration to senior Mazda managers in the US, the little roadster got the green light for production and a drop-top legend was born.

Launched at the Chicago Motor Show in February 1989, the first 'NA' model was powered by a DOHC 1.6-litre, four-cylinder engine codenamed B6-ZE. It produced 115bhp,

power was sent to the rear wheels via a five-speed manual gearbox – connected to the differential by a frame for rigidity – and there were double wishbones at each corner for superb handling. Manual steering was a hasty addition to a car that was designed for power assistance from the outset.

In 1994, a more powerful 1.8-litre engine (code-named BP-ZE) was added, boasting 131bhp, although the output of the 1.6 dropped to a slightly feeble 88bhp. At the same time extra bracing improved body rigidity and there were tweaks to the brakes and interior. The Mark 2 'NB' model arrived in 1998, doing away with those lovely pop-up headlights.

Repairing the rusty windscreen surround

One of the most obvious issues with the MX-5 was the rust that had begun to attack the windscreen surround, or A-pillars. There was serious rust on both sides (just one repair would be shown in the episode, but as with many of the projects there was far more work to do than first appeared), as well as on the scuttle panel beneath the windscreen. And although the offside pillar hadn't looked too bad from a distance, examined up close in the workshop it was clear that it was more than just surface corrosion and would need to be sorted properly.

Preparation

There was plenty to do before any actual rust repairs could start, commencing with removing the windscreen. As it was bonded into place Edd decided to bring in a professional to do the job – it could be a tricky task, and there was a danger of breaking the screen if it was done wrong. Although the cost was modest (just £75), it had to be remembered that the same amount would need to be spent when it came to refitting the screen. More pressure on the already tight budget, then.

Next up was removing both of the front wings, and with the car on the ramp the front wheels and wheel-arch liners were removed. Although a slightly fiddly job, it was going to be a bit easier for poor old Edd as the wings were bolted rather than welded into place. So wielding the screwdrivers and socket set, he removed all of the screws around the nosecone and pop-up headlights; then it was the turn of the bolts that secured the wing to the door pillar and the inner wing seam beneath the bonnet, not forgetting the final bolt at the leading edge of the wing behind the nosecone. With the wiring for the side indicator repeaters disconnected, the wings could be lifted off and carefully stored out of harm's way. The final job was unbolting the bonnet from its hinges, and this too was stored to one side.

Repairing the nearside A-pillar and the scuttle panel

There was a lighter area of corrosion that could be tackled fairly easily on the scuttle panel just below the windscreen on both sides. The rust was just on the surface, so hadn't penetrated too deeply, so the first step was to use an orbital sander to grind away the paint and any loose flakes of rust. With

A common MX-5 problem area that would require all of Edd's body repair skills to remedy.

Before the rust could be tackled, the front wings needed to come off. The ones on the MX-5 simply bolt on.

Removing the bonnet improved access and the windscreen was removed as well.

Applying rust remedy was an effective way to tackle the less serious areas of corrosion.

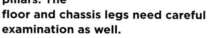

Buying one

➜ **A key factor is rust, so pay particular attention to the wings, wheel arches, sills and windscreen pillars. The floor and chassis legs need careful examination as well.**

➜ **Unless neglected the twin-cam engine is very reliable, but ensure servicing hasn't been skimped and that cambelt changes have been done on time.**

➜ **Suspension and brake systems are trouble-free, but avoid cars without power steering. It ruins the agility, and they aren't more 'pure' to drive, despite what some people say.**

➜ **You need to check the hood and operating mechanism for damage, as water leaks will damage the interior and can allow rust to set in.**

➜ **Plenty of aftermarket parts are available, though these are down to personal taste. And don't be afraid of imported 'Eunos' models just ensure the mods to make them road-legal have been done.**

the areas cleaned of any dust, rust remedy was applied to the affected parts and left to dry. Once it had turned black he knew it had done its work, and the area would be ready for a light skim of filler to remove any pitting. Then a coat of grey primer was applied using an aerosol can.

Cutting and welding the offside A-pillar

Although both windscreen pillars were suffering badly from rot, it was the offside repair that would be tackled on the show. This was much the bigger job of the two, and would certainly require all of Edd's skills if he was to end up with a strong and invisible repair. Donning the goggles and ear defenders again, a grinder and cutting disc was used to carefully cut out the rusty section of metal, removing just the amount needed to take the area back to solid metal. It was important to measure before cutting, as he certainly didn't want to remove any more fresh metal than strictly necessary.

With that done a fresh piece of steel would be needed, for which the trusty paper template method was used, Edd carefully folding it around the A-pillar to get the perfect shape. Using the template a repair section was cut from sheet steel. Good advice given here was to practise a few times beforehand, and not to worry if the paper template and steel cutting required a few attempts – far better to practise now than to ruin the job itself. Happy with the basic shape, some bends and folds were needed so that it exactly followed the shape of the original metal – a solidly mounted vice, some grips and a heavy piece of iron did the job perfectly. Any minor discrepancies could be tapped out with a hammer once the new metal was welded in.

In fact that was the next stage, so Edd used clamps to hold the repair section firmly in place while he applied some initial tack welds using the MIG

Edd made a paper template before forming new metal for the repair section.

MIG welding was required, but it needed to be done slowly to prevent heat distortion damaging surrounding metalwork.

welder. It was done gently, though, as he was keen to avoid any heat distortion that would ruin the finished job. Happy with the positioning of the new section, he used the MIG to apply a continuous weld to finish the job; and if things were a bit messy, well, that didn't matter too much, as any excess weld would be ground off in the next stage.

Finishing the rust repairs and painting

With the new metal in place Edd used a grinding disc to remove excess weld and rubbed back the surrounding paintwork to bare metal in preparation

for the final stage of the job. A perfect finish was needed, so it was important not to rush this part. The next step was to apply a thin layer of filler to the repair – once again a golfball-size of filler to a pea of hardener, as per the instructions. When it was completely dry the filler was rubbed back using a sanding pad. Then it was time to go over the paint that remained on the windscreen surround with a scouring pad, to provide a 'key' for the new paint.

With the area wiped with 'pre-paint' to remove dust and other contaminants, and the windscreen aperture and surrounding bodywork carefully

It took a bit of effort but the new metal is a perfect fit and ready for the next stage.

A thin skim of filler removes any imperfections. It's worth taking time on this for the perfect finish.

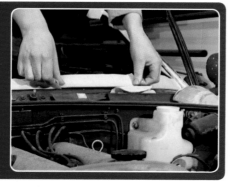
As always, masking the area takes time and patience but it's an important stage to prevent damaging overspray.

Both sides got a coat of primer. Fine wet-and-dry paper can be used to achieve a perfectly smooth surface.

There was no need for the spray booth as careful spraying by hand would give a good finish.

A coat or two of 'Mariner Blue' paint and the job is finished. It looks superb too.

masked using brown paper and tape to prevent overspray, a layer of primer was applied using an aerosol can. Once the primer had dried it was a matter of using 800-grade wet-and-dry paper and a little water to get a perfectly smooth finish so that the surface was ready for its final coat of paint. The colour to be used was 'Mariner Blue', and covering a relatively small area meant there was no need for a trip to the paint shop, Edd preferring instead to apply nice even coats using an aerosol can. It wasn't shown on screen, but a couple of attempts were needed as the original paint mix wasn't quite right, leaving the colour looking rather more purple than it should have done, but it was easily sorted. Job done, and the repair looked superb, the time taken concentrating on the details really paying off with an excellent finish.

Refitting

The final task on the bodywork was to refit the parts that had been removed so Edd could fix the rust. The professional windscreen fitter was brought back to bond the original screen into place and with that job done the wings were carefully bolted back on. Again it was fairly straightforward, although Edd

did take the time to ensure the fit and panel gaps were spot on – some minor adjustment may have been needed before the mounting bolts were finally tightened; and he remembered to reconnect the wiring for the indicator repeaters. With the bonnet bolted back in place, the little roadster was rust-free at last.

Refurbishing the interior

Replacing the damp and scruffy trim

One problem that Mike had noticed when he went to view the car was the damp and musty interior, potentially an issue with any older convertible. The torn hood had allowed water to leak inside, leaving behind some mouldy trim and an unpleasant smell, and it just had to be fixed. Time, then, for some interior renovation.

The first job Edd tackled was removing the seats by undoing the two front and two rear mounting bolts and lifting them from the car. They were past saving so were headed for the skip, and the carpets were next, with a quite a few sections of interior trim needing to be removed first. Items such as

The smelly seats were the next to go and were only fit for the bin.

To remove the carpets the sill trims were unscrewed. Edd made sure he stored all the fittings carefully.

Removing the console is a fiddly but otherwise simple task as long as you take it slowly.

Water leaks in convertibles can rot the floor but luckily this one was in perfect condition.

the driver's footrest were unbolted, the sill trims were unscrewed, and then the centre console was removed – not a difficult task, as it was only secured by various screws, but it did need to be done carefully to avoid damaging any fragile plastic. Those screws needed to be stored away safely too, Edd advising viewers to label screws and clips so they'd know exactly where they went back. Electrical wiring had to be disconnected too (such as the plugs for the electric window switches and hazard warning light switch) and the gear knob removed before the console could be withdrawn.

With everything removed, the front and rear carpets were pulled out. These too were destined straight for the bin. It was a good chance for Edd to examine the floorpan to make sure that the water leaks hadn't allowed rust to take hold, but the MX-5 was fine so it was on with the refurbishment. Keeping a close eye on the budget, Edd had wisely taken the second-hand route and sourced replacement carpets and seats for around £150. Matching the original design and in good condition, they were soon fitted and the nasty smell had been banished.

The carpets were heading for the bin too. At least the cabin wouldn't smell any more.

Edd sourced some second-hand seats in good condition and they just bolted straight in.

Fitting some trim upgrades

While Edd was busy in the workshop Mike had been on a shopping trip, visiting a specialist to buy a range of parts that would upgrade the MX-5 both mechanically and cosmetically. The engine and suspension mods would come later, but Mike's haul also included a variety of chrome-effect parts that he promised would lift the interior ambience. Not that Edd was entirely convinced, but fitting them would thankfully prove straightforward.

The first bits to be applied were shiny chrome surrounds for the dashboard air vents and switches and the interior door handles. The kit came complete with handy alcohol wipes that were used to clean the area; then all that was needed was to peel off the backing and carefully stick the self-adhesive parts in place. Tasteful metal trims for the gear and handbrake levers were next, and these screwed and slid straight on. Then it was time for the stainless-steel MX-5-branded kick plates that would liven up the door sills. All Edd needed to do was to wipe the sill area with pre-paint to remove any dirt, and then use the double-sided sticky tape provided to fix the new trims in place. Once finished, Edd did at

▲ There is a huge range of upgrade parts available for the MX-5, including items such as these chrome roll hoops.

Mike bought some chrome trim to brighten up the cabin, although Edd wasn't convinced at first.

An alcohol wipe removes any grease and then the new trim sticks straight on. Easy.

There's no doubt about it, the original MX-5 is an absolutely cracking little convertible, and if you're looking for some cheap fun, this is the car to be looking at. There are so many around that you won't have trouble finding a good one, and as long as it's not suffering from rot or been abused it should be cheap to run as well. We were really keen to get one on the show but as always the budget was pretty tight, and to be honest the car I bought needed more work than I thought. The hood and interior were a disaster, but I didn't have much choice but to just leave it with Edd and hope he could sort it all in the time we had. Like lots of the cars on *Wheeler Dealers*, both of us ended up burning the midnight oil on this one. It was a real team effort as always.

These lovely metal sill trims were the finishing touch for the interior, and are secured by double-sided tape.

The sporty mesh grille was only a five-minute job for Edd, and just bolted in place.

Various hoses and pipes needed to be removed before the performance air filter could be fitted.

The new filter bolted straight to the airflow meter. The old filter housing can be junked.

least admit that the new parts looked good, so a thumbs-up for Mike!

There were just two more jobs to do before Edd got busy with the mechanicals. Mike's kit of new parts had included a chrome grille for the air intake below the front bumper, for which no modifications were needed; with the mountings screwed into place on the bumper moulding the new grille just clipped into place. Finally there was a new aerial to screw into the rear wing to replace the damaged original.

Fitting the performance air filter

Removing and disassembling the standard air filter

The show was always keen to add value to their modern classic projects, and that often meant improving the way a car drove and handled. Extra performance was always welcome, and the Mazda would come in for some fettling in the form of an air filter upgrade that would add a little extra pep as well as a lovely rorty induction noise.

With an upgrade kit ordered, Edd's first job was to remove the existing arrangement, including the air cleaner housing and the airflow meter, a simple toolkit being more than enough to handle the task. First off was undoing the jubilee clips that secured the inlet and outlet trunking, and then the wiring plug for the airflow meter could be disconnected. Just a few bolts secured the whole arrangement in the engine bay, and with these removed it was a simple matter of undoing the bolts that attached the airflow meter to the air cleaner housing.

Fitting the new parts

Edd started by bolting the airflow meter to the new filter assembly, making sure the cork gasket

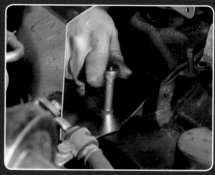

A heat shield was part of the kit and bolted into the holes for the original air filter housing.

Reconnecting the hoses was a bit of a struggle, but a dash of washing-up liquid acted as a lubricant.

Oiling the filter element traps more dust and debris and just needs doing on a regular basis.

Mike's right, the MX-5 was in a real state, and sorting the hood and interior took absolutely hours. And the A-pillar rust was pretty serious too. All in all this one definitely needed some hard work putting in. And I wasn't convinced about some of the modifications Mike had planned, especially the cosmetic stuff, but I guess it looked quite good in the end. Having said that, they are quite easy cars to work on, and things like the bolt-on front wings make some of the jobs easier. There are loads of aftermarket parts available, and as long as you stick to good quality parts they usually bolt straight on without the need for any fettling.

supplied in the kit had been properly located. Reconnecting the original air outlet pipe to the airflow meter proved a bit of a struggle, but as always Edd provided a handy tip, which involved applying a bit of washing-up liquid to the joint to act as a lubricant.

The upgrade kit came with everything needed to fit the parts securely in the MX-5s engine bay, including support brackets for the airflow meter that bolted into the original mounting holes, and a metal heat shield that would protect the filter and airflow meter from any damaging under-bonnet temperatures. These were easy to bolt into place ready for the new parts to be fitted. Before that, however, the new foam filter element got a spray of the oil that was included in the kit, and which would act as extra protection for the engine by trapping even more dirt and grit. One of the benefits of the new filter was that, unlike the disposable paper element fitted as standard, the foam filter could be washed and given a further spray of oil. So not only was it more efficient but it would save money come servicing time too – a classic *Wheeler Dealers* modification!

All that was left was to bolt the new unit to the support brackets, reconnect all of the pipework

– making sure the jubilee clips were properly tightened – and reconnect the plug at the airflow meter. The new filter would certainly help the engine breathe more easily, and, as hoped, added a nice extra rasp to the induction noise.

Fitting the suspension braces

Mike and Edd knew that the now rust-free Mazda looked good, and was going to perform well too, but it never hurt to improve the already impressive handling. So Mike's shopping trip had included a

The front bracing strut bolts into existing holes in the chassis, so a nice easy job for Edd.

It's the same at the rear. A couple of bolts and it's job done on the suspension.

The 'Enkei' alloy rims were second-hand, and really improve the appearance of the little Mazda.

pair of suspension braces that would bolt to the chassis at the front and rear and provide added strength and rigidity to the little soft-top. And that had to be good news.

Both items were simple for Edd to fit, the front brace bolting into existing holes in the chassis members located either side of the gearbox housing. It was just as easy at the back, a bolt at each end securing the brace to the rear chassis legs. Job done, and the result was an even better-handling MX-5.

Some new wheels

The little roadster was almost done, but there was just time for one last cosmetic upgrade to provide the finishing touch to this cracking sports car: a set of replacement alloy wheels. Not that there was anything really wrong with the Minilite-style items fitted as standard, but they were looking a bit tired, so rather than spend time and money refurbishing them some lovely 15in 'Enkei' rims were bolted on instead, second-hand items that had come complete with tyres. In white, they looked terrific against the blue paintwork. And, with a final warning from Edd to get the tracking checked after such modifications (to avoid uneven tyre wear), the MX-5 was finished.

Job done

It had been a long journey, transforming the classic Mazda from a tired, unloved and slightly shabby – not to mention smelly – car into a smart two-seater that was absolutely perfect for summer B-road motoring. The cabin and exterior had been transformed with some tasteful upgrades, the rust had been banished, and the car drove better too. Mike and Edd had pulled it off again, and the sparkling MX-5 sold for a healthy £3,600. Top work!

Final road test

It was still quite early in the life of *Wheeler Dealers* so the test drives were quite modest affairs, but that didn't mean there wasn't an opportunity to give the restored MX-5 a thorough workout. So with the roof down and Mike donning his sunglasses it was time to hit the country lanes and find out whether all their work had paid off. And of course it had. Edd had cracked it yet again and the little roadster felt fantastic, and perfectly at home on the twisty roads.

Peugeot 205 GTI

© Peugeot

Back in 1984, when the 205 GTI was launched, the hot hatchback was big business. There were plenty of talented rivals on the market including the Volkswagen Golf GTI and Ford's Escort XR3i, so bringing something special to the class was going to be a challenge. But the French manufacturer pulled it off in some style, slotting fizzing four-cylinder engines into the pretty 205 body shell to create a car that has since been voted the best hot hatch around. Original models boasted a 105bhp 1.6-litre engine, but it was the later 1.9-litre cars that were to prove popular with buyers after maximum performance, the 130bhp unit being capable of getting the pretty hatch to 60mph in just 7.6 seconds and on to 127mph.

The show had to have one then, and Mike had his eye on the most powerful version of all, the cracking 1.9-litre GTI. With a budget of £2,000 to buy and restore the car, he was looking for an honest example that had seen better days, but while the classified ads had plenty of 1.6-litre models there weren't many 1.9s. His perseverance paid off, though, as he found a tidy-looking and original 1990 model on offer for £1,295, and first impressions were promising. The car looked quite good, but Mike spotted a few issues straight away, including rear suspension that didn't appear quite right, an interior that was in need of smartening up and a few other cosmetic issues.

A check of the engine showed it was leak-free and there were no signs of crash damage, Mike pointing out the different colour bonnet slam panel that was a feature of the model and not necessarily indicative of a previous repair. The test drive revealed an honest example that definitely had potential. Sloppy

Jobs to be tackled

The problem with the gear linkage was going to be the first job on the list. The rear suspension was sitting at the wrong height, so that would be another major task. The 205 would also need some work on the engine, including replacement of the cambelt and fitting a new water pump. Then with the oily bits sorted Edd could get on with tidying the interior and giving the car an external makeover – replacing damaged bumpers and light units – that would see it return to showroom condition.

First step in sorting the sloppy gearchange was assessing the state of the various linkages.

It was the balljoint mounted on the subframe that was the cause of the problem.

Accessing the securing nut was a bit tricky, but otherwise this was an easy fix for Edd.

The new linkage rods just clip on to the balljoints, and the result is a properly sharp gear change again.

gear selection and an odd feel from the back end showed there was work to be done, but neither problem was serious enough to put Mike off, and after handing over £1,000 the little 205 was theirs. Breaking down on the drive back to the workshop wasn't a good omen – the problem, according to Mike and Edd, being leaking hydraulic fluid spilling on to the hot exhaust – but plenty of hours' work would see the cracking hot hatch looking and driving as good as new.

Fixing the gear linkage

Assessing the problem

Having already broken down Edd feared that major work and expense was about to be needed, so the first task was to get the car up on the ramp and assess the problem. Thankfully it wouldn't turn out to be a serious one, as examination of the linkage rods from the gear lever to the gearbox revealed something was amiss. There were two rods to check: the first, controlling the fore and aft movement, was fine, but the second linkage, which looked after the right/left movement, was very loose; so that was clearly the issue here. Closer examination revealed that the GTI had succumbed to a common problem where the linkage ball joint located on the front subframe had come adrift. With a new set of linkages ordered Edd could set about refurbishing the whole arrangement to make sure the gear change was as sharp as you'd expect.

Fitting the new linkages

The first task was to disconnect both of the linkage rods, an easy job as these would just pop off from their ball joints with the help of a small pry bar. With those removed Edd could take a look at the troublesome ball joint on the front subframe, and with it unbolted it was clear that a previous repair had been done incorrectly. An extra nut had been added, meaning the ball joint wasn't correctly seated and therefore moved around, the excess play causing the linkage rod to become detached. Refitting it was a fairly simple job, although access was slightly tricky as the nut holding the joint in place was reached via a hole in the subframe. But with it properly fixed in place – with just one washer and securing nut this time – and the ball joint sockets greased to allow them to pop back into place more easily and prevent future wear, the new linkages could be pushed into place using hand pressure, and the job was finished. The GTI had a sharp and accurate gear change once again.

Changing the cambelt

Accessing and removing the old cambelt

Buying any used car with a patchy service history is a risk, especially if the engine uses a cambelt for valve timing, and the Peugeot was no different. Edd had already spotted that the top cover for the cambelt was missing, so that would need to be

How much did it cost?

Car	£1,000
Gear linkage	£36
Body trim	£240
Exhaust system	£130
Cambelt and water pump	£77
Detailing	£170
Total	*£1,653*

becoming trapped in the fast-spinning belt – and without knowing when the belt itself was last changed fitting a new one was a sensible move.

▼ With a turbocharged engine mounted amidships and four-wheel drive, the 205 T16 was a success in Group B rallying thanks to drivers including the legendary Ari Vatanen. *(Peugeot)*

Before tackling the cambelt, various parts such as the alternator needed to be removed.

Because of the way the engine is installed in a 205 GTI changing the cambelt was a slightly tricky job – Edd had already advised that it wasn't a task to treat lightly on any car – but it wasn't going to defeat him. As always there was some preparation required before he could tackle the job properly, so the car was raised on the ramp (a jack and axle stands could be used instead) so the offside front wheel could be removed. With that out of the way, the access/observation panel in the inner wing was easily removed by undoing a few bolts. The alternator drivebelt would need to come off first, so working

from the top of the engine the alternator mounting bolts were slackened and the belt discarded. It was looking perished, so the safest thing to do was to replace it.

Undoing the securing bolt for the alternator pulley on the crankshaft was next, and with that out of the way Edd could set to work removing the 11mm bolts that secured the lower cambelt cover. Before going any further, however, it was important to ensure that the valve timing marks were correctly aligned. On the GTI they were located on the crankshaft pulley and crankcase and on the camshaft pulley and the mounting for the (missing) top cover. Getting this wrong would prove disastrous when the engine was started after the new belt was fitted, with the potential for valves and pistons to meet with expensive consequences. So as usual, Edd had a top tip: refitting the alternator pulley bolt was a handy way of enabling the engine to be rotated using a suitable socket or spanner. With that done the alignment marks were properly positioned.

Even though Edd was finding the cramped access a bit difficult things were going well so far. Now it was up to the top of the engine for the next job, slackening the belt tensioner and removing the old belt.

Unbolting the lower cambelt cover gives access to the pulleys and tensioner.

It's vital to check the timing marks are aligned before removing the belt if engine damage is to be avoided.

Using a socket on the crank pulley is the best way of rotating the engine to ensure the marks align.

Don't forget to check the top timing marks too, shown here at the camshaft pulley.

Fitting the new cambelt and water pump

The cambelt was clearly in need of replacement, but before the new one could be fitted there was another job to tackle. The water pump on the GTI was driven by the same belt – a common arrangement on many cars – and it's not unusual for the extra tension of a new belt to put stress on a tired pump and cause it to fail. So, not wanting to have to do the whole job again, Edd elected to replace the pump as well. He was prepared for some water loss as the old unit was removed, so a handily positioned container prevented the old coolant from covering the workshop floor. With that sorted the plastic cover over the water pump could be unbolted, followed by the bolts for the pump itself. A small pry bar helped ease the pump away from its joint with the engine block, and with the mounting face on the engine block cleaned of any remaining gasket material, and a smear of sealant added around the edge of the pump housing, the new unit was soon bolted into place.

With that job complete it was just a case of fitting the new cambelt (ensuring the alignment marks were still correct), replacing the missing top

It's worth changing the water pump at the same time, and a new one is cheap to buy.

The old water pump needs carefully levering away, but have a container handy to catch the coolant spillage.

Exterior plastic trim

If you're looking to buy a modern classic, remember to examine the condition of any plastic exterior trim. While it might appear a cheaper and easier fix than chrome parts, in reality many parts are getting rare, and you may need to hunt for second-hand items if the ones on your project are badly damaged. Again, owners' clubs and specialists are a good source of parts, and advice on obtaining them, but there is scope for renovation if necessary. Cracked bumpers can be repaired with heat treatments and flexible filler, and there are various companies out there that can repair minor damage including scuffs and scrapes, as well as repainting localised areas.

© Peugeot

A common problem is black trim that has faded. While replacement may be the only option there are plenty of reasonably priced products available from motor factors that promise to restore the original colour. Some work better than others, and it can be a labour-intensive job, so it's worth trying a few different products until you find one that suits. And don't forget that if you intend to paint plastic trim parts you'll need to use suitable primer and paint that is more flexible than normal and won't crack as the part flexes.

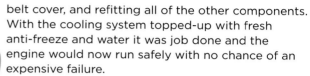

Buying one

➜ **The bodyshells were galvanised from 1987 but you still need to check for rot in the panels, floorpan, suspension mountings and screen surrounds. Crash damage is common too, while exterior trim parts are very hard to source.**

➜ **Ensure the cambelt has been changed on time, and check for signs of a leaking head gasket, worn valve stem oil seals causing exhaust smoke, and airflow meter problems causing rough running.**

➜ **Failed rear suspension radius arm bearings ruin the rear axle if left unchecked, so inspect them carefully. Brakes are trouble-free, but ensure the ABS system on later cars is working properly – it's an MOT failure if it's not.**

➜ **Interiors are fragile so watch for cracked dashboards, general wear and tear and electrical woes. Sourcing replacement trim is likely to mean a hunt for second-hand parts.**

➜ **Modified cars are common and not everyone's cup of tea. Check you're happy with the standard of any work, and remember that original ones fetch the best money.**

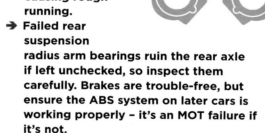

belt cover, and refitting all of the other components. With the cooling system topped-up with fresh anti-freeze and water it was job done and the engine would now run safely with no chance of an expensive failure.

While Edd was under the bonnet he also took the opportunity to replace a faulty cold start valve in the fuel injection system. Although it wasn't actually shown in the programme, it was clearly a repair that was needed to keep the GTI's engine in perfect health.

Sourcing some replacement parts

With Edd putting in the hours at the workshop, Mike was out on the road on the hunt for replacement interior trim parts. With the tight budget – and future profit – in mind he headed for a breaker's yard, where he found a perfect donor car from which to salvage a few important parts. A bit of haggling and just £45 later he was the proud owner of a replacement steering wheel, gear knob and parcel shelf. They were all in good condition and it was a useful haul of bits that Edd could fit later in the project.

As Mike discovered, this battered looking thing is a treasure trove of spare parts.

The haul from the scrapyard. These parts cost just a few pounds, helping to keep the restoration budget down.

Fixing the rear axle

Assessing the problem

One of the problems that Mike had noticed straight away when he went to view the car was that the rear wheels didn't appear to be correctly positioned in the wheel-arches. They looked to be mounted a little too far back, so something was clearly amiss, and the poor ride quality experienced on the test drive confirmed it. Indeed, it was just the sort of issue that Mike always looked for when buying a car like this, as it was the sort of thing that could indicate a car with problems elsewhere. If the suspension was awry, what else might be wrong? Not that there was time to worry about such things, as it was over to Edd for him to work his magic...

What he found was that the ride height at the rear of the car had been lowered, a popular modification on cars like these but one that doesn't always work so well on the road. The design of the 205's rear suspension meant that the height could be adjusted by raising or lowering the rear suspension arms and then rotating the torsion bar springs before locking them in place. It was clear

▲ Does the 205 look better in red or white? You decide, but either way this is a cracking hot hatchback. *(Peugeot)*

that the arrangement would need to be returned to its original factory setting, so that was the next task to be tackled.

Resetting the ride height

The first step was to gain proper access to the suspension, so the entire exhaust system was removed. With the clamp bolts undone, the rear silencer box was separated from the rest of the system. Working at the front of the car, the bolts securing the downpipe to the exhaust manifold were undone. Then it was just a matter of unhooking the rubber mountings and lowering the system out of the way. It was a system that had seen better days too – Edd had already noticed that it was corroded in a few areas, with a few small holes appearing, so a new exhaust was added to the parts list.

With that job done, the lower shock absorber mountings were unbolted so that the units could be moved to one side, the spare wheel was released from its carrier to give extra room, and the handbrake cables were unclipped from the

The old exhaust was blowing and was only fit for the scrap heap.

Changing the exhaust on the 205 is a DIY task and only requires a basic toolkit.

▼ While Mike went for the more powerful 1.9-litre model, the 205 was launched with a 1.6 engine boasting 105bhp. *(Peugeot)*

Before sorting the ride height, the shock absorber lower mount needs to be undone.

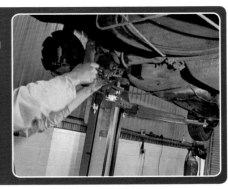

The shock absorber can just be pulled out of the way to give access to the rest of the suspension components.

suspension arms. There was now clear access to the main components of this particular job, the torsion bars. Removing them was going to be the first challenge, and with the splined mountings in the suspension arms showing signs of surface corrosion they weren't going to come out easily. A special tool was needed in the shape of a slide hammer, an ideal piece of kit for exerting the force needed to extract the springs. With the hammer securely attached to the end of the torsion bar a bit of effort soon saw them released from the suspension arm and chassis.

The next step was establishing the correct ride height. Using workshop data, Edd found that an extra 40mm of height would need to be added to return the car to its factory setting. Taking exact measurements on both sides of the car was going to be vital if he wasn't to end up with a lopsided hot hatch, so he took careful measurements between the top of the wheel-arch and the centre point of the wheel hub.

Before the torsion bars were replaced – ensuring they were replaced on their original sides, as swapping them could lead to handling issues – the splines at each end were cleaned and coated with grease to make refitting easier. This would also prevent them seizing in place in the future. It was then just a case of pulling down on each suspension assembly until the desired ride height was reached (doing this effectively increased the distance between the wheel hub and bodywork, so increasing the ride height), and tapping the torsion bars back into their mountings to lock everything firmly in place. To finish the job the lower mountings for the shock absorbers were bolted back in place, making sure they were done up to the correct torque, and the new exhaust system was fitted – an easy job requiring just a basic toolkit.

After a dose of penetrating fluid, Edd gets to work with a slide hammer to remove the torsion bars.

Careful measurement establishes the correct ride height before adjusting the suspension arms and refitting the torsion bars.

Fitting the new exhaust is a quick job for Edd, then the 205 will sound perfect once again.

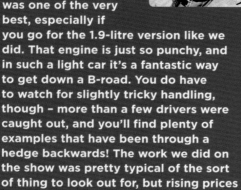

I've always been a huge fan of the hot hatchback, and I bought and sold plenty back in my trading days. And I reckon the 205 GTI was one of the very best, especially if you go for the 1.9-litre version like we did. That engine is just so punchy, and in such a light car it's a fantastic way to get down a B-road. You do have to watch for slightly tricky handling, though – more than a few drivers were caught out, and you'll find plenty of examples that have been through a hedge backwards! The work we did on the show was pretty typical of the sort of thing to look out for, but rising prices mean there is real investment potential here and you'll absolutely love it.

It's important to align the front wheels before fitting the new steering wheel, so it's not crooked afterwards.

That nasty aftermarket steering wheel had to go; just a few screws secure it to the boss.

After lowering the car to the ground and checking that both sides were at exactly the same height, the wheels were perfectly positioned within the wheel-arches – meaning that Edd had cracked this particular task, and the 205 now sat perfectly on the road just as Peugeot intended.

Renovating the interior

When Mike had bought the car it was clear that a few interior jobs would need doing if the GTI was going to look its best. The condition was good on the whole, but there were a few items that were letting things down, and if the best sale price was going to be reached, those jobs would need to be tackled. The parts he'd bought from the scrapyard were about to prove very handy indeed.

Replacing the steering wheel

Buyers often want cars like these to be as original as possible, so the aftermarket steering wheel would have to go. The replacement would be the lovely leather-bound three-spoke item that the GTI had when new, so the first job was to remove the current one. Before starting work, though, Edd made sure that the front wheels were completely straight, otherwise he'd end up with a crooked steering wheel when driving down the road.

The old wheel was attached to the boss by six screws, which were easily removed, Then the bolt that secured the boss to the steering column could be undone. The boss itself put up a bit of a fight but it was soon parted from the column, and after a final check that the front wheels were properly aligned the replacement wheel was bolted in place, making sure the securing bolt was tightened to the correct torque. With the GTI badge pressed into place, the cabin was already looking much better.

Replacing the gear knob, floor mats and parcel shelf

A new set of floor mats were easy to fit and really lifted the interior. Likewise, the tatty old gear knob pulled straight off and the second-hand part was pushed into place. With the interior nearly finished, the last job was fitting the new parcel shelf. The old one had had holes cut out for aftermarket hi-fi speakers, so that would have to go. The only problem was that the replacement Mike had found was from a car with a grey interior. Theirs was black.

But no matter, as a slightly cheeky fix was in order. Edd simply applied a few coats of black paint from an aerosol can, and the parcel shelf now looked as good as new. It had been an effective and very cheap fix. And just to finish off the interior, although not shown in the programme, a new radio/CD player was slotted into the dash to fill the gaping hole.

Replacing the exterior trim

With the mechanical work and interior sorted, the project was coming together. However, there were a few other cosmetic issues that were letting things down, so these were the last jobs to get the Edd China treatment.

Wheel-arch trims and bumpers

Over the years fragile parts like these can become scuffed and damaged, and as only the best would do for a *Wheeler Dealers* car the

▼ The 205 GTI was also available as a convertible, but it was known as the CTI instead. It was just as much fun as the regular hatchback. *(Peugeot)*

One of Mike's car dealing tips! A can of black paint soon has the parcel shelf matching the interior.

You'd never know the difference! The finished shelf looks great and was just a cheap second-hand part.

◄ Dark grey was another popular choice for GTI buyers. (Peugeot)

decision was taken to give the exterior of the 205 a makeover. What viewers didn't see, though, were the hours that Mike and Edd spent experimenting with various different trim treatments designed to restore its faded plastic parts, until it became clear that those on the project car were too far gone, and that only new items would bring back that showroom look. As Edd explained, it probably would have been possible to source everything they needed second-hand, but new parts were just £240 so that was a much quicker and easier route. He also warned that doing these jobs could turn out to be pretty fiddly, so allowing a whole day for the work would be best.

The first thing to do was remove the grey plastic trims over each wheel arch, which were held on by a variety of screws and clips. There was a warning here though, which is that the clips in this case were riveted to the body panels, so care was needed during removal to ensure the rivets weren't pulled out as well. The side rubbing strips were also removed. Again they were just clipped into position, but the red inserts were prised from place first. While care was needed not to damage the bodywork – a proper trim removal tool is ideal, rather than using a screwdriver – the trims themselves were going to be replaced, so a bit of damage to those would be fine.

Next up was bumper removal, as new ones were ready to be fitted. With the red inserts removed and the front fog light wiring disconnected, the front and rear bumpers were unbolted from their mounting points. There was time for a top tip before refitting the new ones: it was good advice

It's quite easy removing the plastic trim, but try to avoid breaking the clips or scratching the paintwork.

If I'm honest I'd probably say that I prefer the Golf GTI as a hot hatch, but it's easy to see why the Peugeot 205 GTI is so popular. The 1.9-litre engine is a great unit, and it's robust if you look after it properly. The 205 isn't too hard to work on either. As a technical exercise Peugeot got the GTI spot on, and – typical of French cars – there are some clever design touches. For example, models fitted with a sunroof got a clever sealing system that used a vacuum pump to expand the seal when the roof was shut, with the pressure released when you opened it. It's a great detail and one that I'd like to have played with on the show, but ours was fine so I didn't need to touch it unfortunately.

as always, and involved checking the metalwork behind the bumpers for any signs of corrosion. As areas that can rust away unseen, now would be the perfect opportunity to address any problems before they get worse.

With everything fine on this particular GTI, the new rear bumper could be bolted in place, replacing the shabby original. However, the front bumper needed a bit more work before it was ready for refitting. Undoing the securing bolts and clips allowed the front spoiler to be separated from the bumper. Then, once it was cleaned up, it could be reattached to the new bumper before the whole lot was bolted back in position, not forgetting to reconnect the wiring for those fog lamps.

By this stage the car was also ready for the new wheel-arch trims and side rubbing strips. These clipped neatly into place, taking care not to damage any of the mounting clips as they were fitted. Finishing everything off were the new red inserts, a new fuel cap (sprayed in the correct body colour using an aerosol can) that was needed to replace the original with its damaged lock, and a new set of number plates to replace the cracked and tatty originals.

Removing the damaged rear bumper was just a case of undoing a few bolts and lifting it away.

With the bumpers removed Edd checked for signs of corrosion behind. This isn't serious and was easily sorted.

Here the original spoiler gets reattached to the new front bumper. The new parts will really lift the look.

Someone had attacked the fuel cap. A replacement was cheap and just needed painting before popping it on.

The damaged rear light lenses just screw on. The easiest job of the whole project for Edd.

It wasn't worth buying second-hand parts as nice shiny new ones were a cheap fix.

Replacing the light units

It wasn't only the plastic trim that was letting down the look of the little GTI, as some of the light lenses were also damaged. The finished car needed to look perfect, so undoing the two screws at the top of each unit soon had each of the rear light lenses removed and replaced with new items. A new front indicator lens was also needed, so the offside front headlamp was removed. Then, working from within the lamp housing, the old indicator unit was unscrewed, and with the bulb wiring disconnected it took Edd just a moment to replace it, refit the headlamp and screw the radiator grille back in place.

Removing the headlight gives access to the broken indicator that needed replacing. It just unscrewed from the wing.

Job done

Mike and Edd had certainly needed to put in the hours on this one, not only fixing some mechanical troubles but also making sure that the superb 205 GTI looked as good as it went. But all that work had paid off. They'd rescued a slightly shabby example and given it a new lease of life, ensuring this fantastic little road rocket would provide plenty of fun motoring for years to come. And looking and driving as well it did it was no surprise that it would soon find a new owner, one that paid £2,200 for one of the best hot hatches ever made.

With the new indicator fitted it's a quick job to replace the headlight, though you might want to check the alignment afterwards.

Final test drive

With a warning from Edd not to overdo it, Mike grabbed the keys and headed for some twisty B-roads to test the sharp handling of this iconic hot hatchback. And it was no surprise to hear him announce that Edd had done an absolutely cracking job yet again. It had been another great transformation from an unloved car to one with all of the attributes you'd expect from a 205 GTI, including a slick gearbox and pin-sharp handling. This was one Peugeot that had been given another lease of life, and it deserved nothing less.

Just the new grille to go on and the 205 is finished!

Porsche 911 Targa

It's amazing to think that this wonderful sports car has been in production for more than 50 years, with every generation improving the recipe for ever greater performance and handling. The 993 generation arrived in the latter part of 1993 and promised to be one of the finest models yet, boasting a stiffer bodyshell, a smooth new look that drew inspiration from the much-admired early cars, and a clever new multi-link rear suspension system for dynamic yet secure handling. It would also be the last outing for the air-cooled flat-six engine, revered by Porsche enthusiasts and considered by many to be the mark of a true 911. The water-cooled cars that followed struggled to gain quite the same affection, and the debate between which is best rages on to this day.

It wasn't the first time that a 911 had entered the *Wheeler Dealers* workshop, but the model had grown increasingly complex so this one would provide Edd with something of a challenge. Mike started by scouring the Internet looking for examples at around £15,000, but he wasn't having any luck – prices are rising fast for this most desirable of 911s – but he did find one for sale from a Porsche specialist. Being sold on behalf of the owner, the asking price was just £13,000, so Mike was quickly on his way to inspect it.

He wasn't entirely delighted with what he found. The 993 had plenty of service history, which is always a good sign, and it was a desirable six-speed manual model, but it had been badly neglected and there was a raft of cosmetic issues that would need to be sorted. The leather cabin trim was looking tired as well, but at least the sliding Targa roof worked fine. Nor was it perfect on the road, feeling down on power and lacking the sharpness

Jobs to be tackled

One of the biggest issues was the seeming lack of power during acceleration – not what you'd expect from a car boasting 285bhp – which was traced to a fault with the Varioram variable intake system. There was also the matter of the tired, noisy suspension that would need major fettling, and a host of cosmetic problems letting the car down. The cabin was tatty, the alloy wheels were in a terrible state, the light units were faded, and the electrically operated rear spoiler wasn't working properly. There was plenty to do then.

The air-conditioning compressor was just one of the many parts requiring removal to gain access to the Varioram system.

With so many vacuum pipes to disconnect, labelling them is a sensible plan.

Edd gets to work dismantling the Porsche's troublesome Varioram induction system. It's a complex bit of kit.

One of the vacuum actuators that operate the system. These were working fine, so the problem lay elsewhere.

expected from a Porsche. However, it was within budget, and with some tough bargaining from Mike it was his for £12,000. Could the boys turn this unloved 911 around? Of course they could...

Diagnosing and fixing the Varioram problem

With the complete system removed Edd was able to explain how it worked. The Varioram induction system used variable-length intakes to boost power and mid-range torque, and worked by effectively altering the length of the inlet pipes depending on engine speed. Below 5,000rpm the intakes were around twice the length of non-Varioram engines, but as engine speed rose vacuum-operated sleeves shortened the pipes for better high-speed breathing.

But Mike had complained that performance was lacking, with the engine feeling like it was 'holding back' as he accelerated. So it needed investigation, and that meant removing the entire induction system from the engine. The job could be done with the engine in situ but Edd would need as much access as possible in the packed engine bay, so his first task was to unbolt and remove the engine compartment lid, secured by two bolts at each hinge. Then he had to disconnect the multitude of wires and vacuum pipes, making sure they were clearly labelled to aid reassembly. A top tip here was to purchase a hand-held label maker that would make the job easier and quicker.

While Edd would try to disturb as few parts as possible there were still plenty of components to remove before the Varioram system could be withdrawn, including disconnection and removal of the induction system pipework and the removal of the air-conditioning compressor (after the refrigerant had been carefully discharged, of course). It was an involved job, with the work taking around four hours. But it was much easier than following the official Porsche method, which was to remove the engine completely, and in fact the boys were so keen not to have to remove the engine that they went against advice here. But it showed that sometimes you can find a shortcut if you think about a job logically.

With the unit on the bench Edd could get on with stripping it down to find the cause of the problem. Nine bolts secured the manifold pipes, and removing them exposed the adjustable Varioram

intakes. Then Edd set to work on testing the system using a small vacuum pump. The system operates via a series of vacuum actuators that are controlled by the engine's main electronic control unit, so operating them manually would reveal what was happening inside.

What Edd found was that once retracted one set of intake rams didn't extend again – clearly the source of the lacklustre performance that Mike had noticed on the test drive. With the pipes removed, closer examination of the operating mechanism revealed that the securing pin for the operating arm had become detached. A new arm was all that was needed, but of course there was a problem. No individual components were available for the

How much did it cost?

Car	£12,000
Wheels and tyres	£820
Suspension	£3,000
Spare parts	£850
Polishing and paint	£850
Total	*£17,520*

The Porsche Targa

© Porsche

The first Porsche 911 Targa arrived back in 1966 and was designed because of rumours that America were about to outlaw full convertibles on safety grounds. Though this legislation never materialised, the Targa (a name trademarked by Porsche for automotive use) has remained a popular 911 variant ever since. Original models had a lift-out section above the passenger compartment, a stainless-steel roll hoop and a folding rear window, but this last arrangement was fiddly, and a fixed glass rear window became optional from 1968 and standard from 1972. The 993 version was the first model to adopt a different approach, with a sliding glass panel – operated by a series of electric motors and cables – replacing the lift-out section. There was also an electric sunblind fitted, while an interlock mechanism ensured that the rear hatch couldn't be lifted when the roof was open.

The system is generally reliable, but the key thing is ensuring that the seals are clean and undamaged and that the roof panel slides correctly. Regular use of a silicone lubricant keeps things healthy, but if the roof section fails to operate or appears to slip or jam then suspect worn motors, stretched cables or failed microswitches.

Varioram system, and Porsche were only prepared to sell a complete unit at significant cost. However, a bit of time spent online secured a second-hand part for just £60 – another great example of how using some ingenuity can save a lot of cash and keep project costs as low as possible.

Removing the broken item was a quick job: carefully unclipping the connecting ball joint on the outside of the casing allowed it to be slid from position. With the new operating arm fitted, a quick test with the vacuum pump revealed that everything was working as it should, and then Edd was ready to put in the hours and refit the system to the engine. It wasn't a job to be rushed – the 993 was a complex car, after all – so his advice was to take as much time as possible to ensure that everything was refitted correctly, especially all of those vacuum pipes that would need careful reconnection. Indeed, getting that aspect right would prove crucial, which was why labelling them was so important, even for a top mechanic like Edd. That way he could ensure that the engine would run perfectly first time and avoid the need for time-consuming extra work. But of course, he'd done a brilliant job as always and the engine was back to the rudest of health. Then, with the engine lid bolted back on to its hinges, it was on to more mechanical work.

Sorting the suspension

One of the issues Mike had spotted on the test drive was suspension that felt past its best – it was noisy, and the 993 lacked the agility and sharpness expected from this legendary sports car. It was time to get the Porsche up on the ramp and see what was what.

What Edd found were dampers that were not only leaking but were also in a poor state overall, with damaged dust covers and corrosion of the damper body. They certainly weren't good enough for the Porsche, so it was clear that new items would be needed. But rather than just replace them with standard items, the boys decided to go all out and get a custom set of adjustable dampers made. It would be a big investment – a hefty £3,000 – but it would make the car more desirable, and therefore saleable. So while Mike was getting them made at a specialist company (they were labour-intensive to construct but would be a real treat for the neglected 911, and

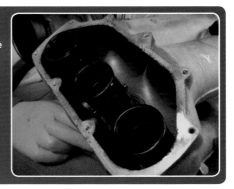

A peek inside the Varioram system. These are variable-length pipes that help boost torque at lower engine speeds.

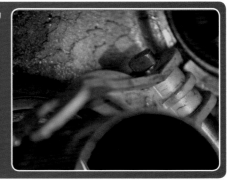

The actuating arm that has been causing the problem. Luckily it's a cheap part.

Reconnecting all the vacuum pipes takes time but the labels prove a huge help. It's a handy tip.

After hours of labour the system is back in place, and the engine is performing as it should.

worth every penny), Edd got on with removing the old units. Starting at the front, he pulled back the carpeting in the front luggage compartment to gain access to the top strut mountings and undid the four securing nuts. After a squirt of penetrating fluid the bottom mounts unbolted at the wheel hub, and the tatty old struts were removed. The process was repeated at the rear, and despite encountering a few corroded fittings the excellent build quality ensured that everything came apart quite easily.

The new front struts had a spherical top mounting rather than the solid rubber of the original items, which would allow various geometry adjustments to be made, including camber. And the rear items were also adjustable, changes being made via a control wired to the dampers and accessed from the engine bay. Delivered to Edd with new springs and the adjustable mountings in place, all that was needed now was to refit them to the 993, ensuring that both upper and lower mounting bolts were done up to the correct torque. The ride height had been adjusted to approximately the right level before fitting, but as Edd pointed out, some further

The clever new dampers were adjustable for the perfect suspension set-up. Expensive, but worth every penny.

The front struts are held in place by four bolts within the front luggage compartment.

Buying one

→ **Stone-chipping around the nosecone is common, while other issues include creaking windscreens, broken door check-straps and corroded bumper mountings. Bodywork repairs aren't cheap, so avoid neglected and abused examples.**

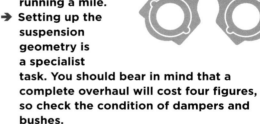

→ **Major engine or gearbox work will result in big bills, so it's best to get them inspected. Oil leaks aren't uncommon, but excessive exhaust smoke should have you running a mile.**

→ **Setting up the suspension geometry is a specialist task. You should bear in mind that a complete overhaul will cost four figures, so check the condition of dampers and bushes.**

→ **Brakes can take a pounding, so check the discs for wear, corrosion and signs of cracks. Again, a complete overhaul is a costly business so haggle accordingly if work is needed.**

→ **Watch for shabby and unloved interiors and make sure all the electrical equipment is working. Ensure the sliding Targa roof operates smoothly, and check for signs of water leaks in the cabin.**

One of the worn anti-roll bar drop links that were the cause of clunking suspension.

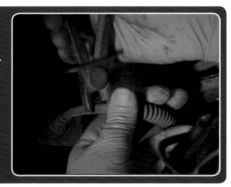

Edd clamps the brake hoses before starting work. Only use the correct tools for this sort of job.

The back plates were completely corroded but replacements from Porsche weren't expensive.

The brake calipers are easy to remove, held on by just a couple of bolts.

adjustment would almost certainly be needed once the new dampers had settled.

If you're not sure of getting the settings correct you could always ask a Porsche specialist to set things up for you. In fact the correct wheel and suspension alignment on a 993 is crucial if it's to handle properly, and it's not an easy task, so don't be tempted to ignore this if you make any suspension modifications. As Edd would tell you, it's easy to bolt on new parts, but the important thing is making sure that they work as they should. If you're not confident about doing the work, don't be afraid to entrust the task to a specialist.

Extra suspension and brake work

While working on the dampers Edd had noticed two more problems that would need attention. Mike had complained that the suspension was noisy, so a check of the ball joints and mountings using a pry bar to move the various parts revealed that the drop links for the front anti-roll bar were worn and needed replacing. It was a simple job, though, with the links just needing to be unbolted from the anti-roll bar and the bottom of the suspension strut. With the securing bolts correctly tightened, there would be no more nasty clunks from the suspension.

But the other issue needing attention was the brakes, specifically the back plates that protected the front discs from muck and road debris. They were badly corroded and almost falling off – not exactly what you'd expect from a Porsche, so they had to go. And while the parts themselves were cheap – original factory parts were just £20 – fitting them would add another few hours to this detailed project. The first stage for Edd was to clamp the flexible brake hose with a proprietary tool, and with that done the two bolts securing the brake caliper to the carrier were undone, the brake pipe was disconnected at the bleed nipple, and the caliper withdrawn.

The brake disc was next, held in place with just a small screw – a squirt of penetrating fluid might sometimes be needed if it's corroded in place. With the disc out of the way it was a simple job to undo the four bolts for the back plates and replace them with shiny new parts. Then all that was left was to refit the brake discs and calipers, ensuring the caliper-to-carrier bolts were correctly torqued, and bleed the brakes.

The brake disc is easily removed, although care is needed to avoid rounding-off the securing screw.

The damaged spoiler quadrant is clearly visible here, missing teeth causing the problem.

The suspension and brakes were now in tip-top condition, but the work wasn't finished yet. There were plenty of other issues to tackle before the 993 would be ready for sale, and the next item needing attention was the rear spoiler.

Repairing the rear spoiler

The 993 generation of this legendary Porsche was fitted with a clever rear spoiler. Rather than being fixed permanently in position like many cars, it extended electrically at 50mph before retracting again at 5mph for the perfect blend of aerodynamics and downforce. But all wasn't well on the *Wheeler Dealers* car. A switch in the cabin at the rear of the centre console allowed the driver to extend and retract the spoiler manually – which was handy for cleaning – but a quick test by Edd revealed that it wasn't operating properly, not rising fully unless pulled up by hand. It was time to strip down the mechanism to investigate.

The first step was to remove the spoiler cover, which was held in place by just a few easily accessible screws, two on each side. With that out

Edd used some tape to ensure the vital spacer didn't go missing.

Removing the spoiler cover is a quick job and gives access to the operating mechanism.

The new quadrant was a cheap part from Porsche, and it all goes back together easily. Problem solved.

To be honest, I was really shocked at the condition of the 911 – I don't think I'd ever seen one as abused as this. But we really wanted to get another one on the show, and to find a 993 for this sort of money was amazing. Both of us loved it, and as soon as I took it for a test drive I knew this was the one. I think I said it on the show, but sometimes you just get a feel about a car that needs rescuing, and this Porsche was one of those. I knew there was a good car underneath so there was no way I was going to let this one go, and I got it for a really good price in the end. We spent some serious money on it but it was definitely worth it.

of the way and the plastic air vent panel unscrewed it was easy to see the operating mechanism, which was secured to the engine lid itself, and it soon became obvious where the problem lay. The spoiler was operated by a motor that connected via a worm drive to a toothed quadrant or rack, and closer examination showed a number of teeth on the rack were missing and damaged, hence the spoiler not being able to extend fully.

Luckily it was possible to buy just the rack from Porsche, so with the new part ordered the old one was carefully removed. It would prove to be a fiddly task with various small clips and screws to be removed, and it was particularly important not to lose the small spacer, so Edd wrapped some tape around it to prevent it disappearing into the depths of the engine bay. The new part fitted easily, although it was important to ensure it was fitted in exactly the right position if the spoiler was to raise effectively. It was therefore advisable to take notes or pictures before starting work.

The final step was adding a bit of extra lubrication by applying graphite from a pencil to the gear drive and rack, this method being preferred because using grease would attract grit and dirt. And with the external cover screwed firmly back in place, a quick test revealed that the spoiler was now working perfectly. It had been a cheap and fairly straightforward fix, but now there was some cosmetic work to attend to.

The cosmetic tasks

Replacing and updating the light units

The rear light units and the reflector between them were faded and damaged, and really letting down the looks of the 993, so, trying to keep the parts spend as low as possible, Edd sourced some second-hand items in good condition. They were easy to remove, the indicator lenses being held in place with a crosshead screw at each end and the reflector panel by screws accessible with the engine cover open. It was then just a case of disconnecting the wiring plugs at the rear of the unit before withdrawing them. But as ever it was important to ensure the Porsche was in top condition, so Edd also took the time to clean the cavity behind the lights before the new ones were fitted. That way if they were removed in future it would be obvious that the car had been looked after, always a good sign for future owners.

There was time for a few upgrades at the front too, Edd unscrewing the fog and indicator lamp units and replacing them with later clear-lensed items for a fresh new look (the old items were left in the car, in case a future owner wanted to return its looks to standard). The headlamps would get upgraded halogen bulbs too, but he gave some advice before doing this, which was to avoid using cheap replacement items. They were often of inferior quality, and spending extra money on good quality bulbs would pay dividends in terms of stronger, sharper light output and longer service life. And his demonstration of what happened if you opted for cheap bulbs was the perfect illustration of why aiming for original equipment standards is always best (something that Edd would tell you applies to many aspects of car restoration.)

The new bulbs were nice and easy to fit, thanks to Porsche's clever arrangement for removing the headlamps. It can be a tricky job on many modern cars, but on the 911 the release mechanism is accessed from within the front luggage compartment. Pulling back the carpet on each side reveals an aperture that accepts a special key to move the locking bar beneath the light unit, and it takes only a moment to withdraw the unit, remove the plastic cover at the rear and replace the bulb (taking care, of course, not to touch the glass surface of the bulb with bare hands, as any oils deposited on the surface cause contamination and can reduce the bulb's service life). It was a typically thoughtful piece of design from Porsche and one that Edd thoroughly appreciated.

Replacing the exhaust tail pipes

Every part of a Porsche should shout quality, and the corroded exhaust pipe tips were letting down

The rear light lenses were faded and damaged, so changing them was the only option.

The new reflector just screwed into place. The parts weren't cheap but really improved the looks.

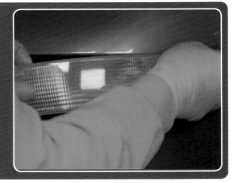

The orange lenses were swapped for later spec items to give the 993 a bit of a facelift.

The new clear-lens light units just screw into place. It's a subtle but effective update.

Refurbishing wheels

No matter what sort of wheels your classic has got – steel, alloy or wire – it will spoil the look of the finished project if they're in tatty condition:

- Steels wheels are the easiest to refurbish. With brake dust and grime removed using a proprietary wheel cleaner, any major corrosion can be tackled using a grinder or coarse wet and dry paper. Specialists can remove any dents or deformation of the rim that's been caused by impact damage. With the surface thoroughly cleaned the wheel can be painted using an aerosol can to massively improve the appearance.
- Alloy wheels can be trickier to renovate

– it's doable on a DIY basis, but there are plenty of specialists that can do the job for around £50–60 per wheel depending on the work required. Special cleaning techniques such as grit blasting or acid dipping can remove old paint and lacquer, leaving the wheels ready for painting or powder coating.
- Refurbishing wire wheels will probably need the skills of a specialist, but the cost shouldn't be prohibitive, and will almost certainly be cheaper than buying new items. Common areas needing attention include replacing rusty and damaged spokes, adjusting the spokes to ensure the wheel runs true, and replacing worn splines and hubs.

Corroded exhaust tips needed to be cut off but the shiny new ones looked great and were easy to fit.

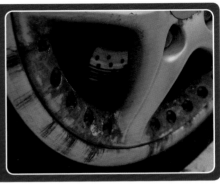

Specialists can refurbish damaged alloys, and these certainly needed attention. It cost £500 for all four.

its appearance. Wearing the proper protective gear – goggles and ear defenders – Edd set to work with the angle grinder to cut off the parts, as the old clamp bolts were too rusty to undo. That done, it was just a moment's work to bolt the shiny new items in place.

The alloy wheels

When the 993 left the factory it was fitted with a set of lovely split-rim alloy wheels, but years of neglect had left them badly corroded and looking in a very sorry state. They were too far gone for Edd to tackle, so the wheels were sent to a specialist to be refurbished at a cost of £500 for all four. They were also fitted with brand new rubber ready to be bolted back on and restore the car's gorgeous looks.

A couple of interior improvements

The luxurious leather-lined cabin hadn't escaped neglect either and was looking very tatty in a few places, so Edd needed to work his magic. Buying new Porsche parts would have seriously dented the budget, so he got to work obtaining a second-hand gear lever and gaiter, and a replacement steering wheel to substitute for the badly damaged original.

With the gaiter unclipped from the centre console the old gear knob just pulled from the lever and the new one was firmly pushed into place and the gaiter secured. Replacing the steering wheel was a bit more involved, and the first step was to remove the centre pad to gain access to the airbag. These can be dangerous to work on unless proper precautions are taken, so the battery was disconnected before starting work, and a few minutes were allowed for any residual current to dissipate. With the wiring disconnected, the air bag was lifted away and stored safely and the securing nut for the wheel was undone. Once Edd had checked to ensure that the front wheels were pointing straight ahead, the replacement wheel was bolted in place and the air-bag unit replaced. It was advisable to ensure no one was in the car when the battery was reconnected and the ignition was

A second-hand steering wheel replaced the tatty original. Care is needed when removing airbags.

'Mopping' the paintwork would bring back the shine, but the paint depth needed checking first.

turned on after replacing the airbag, just in case it should activate unexpectedly. It was all fine, though, and the cabin was looking worthy of the marque once more.

Renovating the paintwork

With the project almost finished there was just one more job to do, and that was to freshen up the tired and faded paintwork. It would need deep polishing to remove the very top layer of paint, and this was done by 'mopping', using a 'motor operated polisher'. The first thing to do, though, was to measure the depth of the paint to ensure it was thick enough for such a job – if it was too thin there was a risk of polishing down to the primer coat, so it needed to be at least 25 microns thick. However, it was fine on the 993, and once polished and with new number plates fitted to replace the cracked originals the Porsche was finished.

Job done

It had been a huge project for Mike and Edd. The 993 had been a bargain, but it had been badly neglected, with a whole lot of work to do if it was to meet the *Wheeler Dealers* standard. But as always they'd pulled it off, and this iconic sports car looked worthy of its Porsche badge once more. Mike reckoned it was worth every penny of £20,000, but after some hard bargaining from the prospective buyer he let it go for just £500 less – a great profit thanks to Edd's hard work, and another superb modern classic given a new lease of life.

Final test drive

The Porsche 911 is a truly wonderful sports car, and only the best driving roads would do for this

test. So it was off to the deserted roads of the Yorkshire Dales, where Mike and Edd could make the very most of that potent flat-six engine. As Mike observed, the new suspension had provided the 911 not only with pin-sharp handling but with a good ride too, so it was the perfect combination for the challenging and undulating tarmac. And having enjoyed the performance on offer, there was just time to meet up with the owners of five generations of this legendary coupe. But with the sun setting and the boys looking a bit chilly it was time to head back to the workshop and get the Porsche sold.

Although the 993 was really poor cosmetically, the biggest job to do was fixing the Varioram system. Porsche's official method is to remove the engine, but that's a major task on one of these, which is why I wanted to see whether it could be done with the engine in place. Sometimes there's no way of avoiding a job however time-consuming, so you can't always look for a shortcut, but on other occasions – like with the Porsche – it's worth just taking some time before you get started to think about whether there is an easier way. Luckily this one worked out, although it still took a good few hours, and it needed a really methodical approach, with all the vacuum pipes involved.

Subaru Impreza WRX

With a punchy turbocharged boxer engine and four-wheel drive the Subaru Impreza WRX really is a rally car for the road, and if you're looking for performance on a budget, there are few better cars. Not only is it quick, but the security of that four-wheel-drive system means it can get its power to the road whatever the weather, and that makes it a very effective way of getting from A to B.

With all of its success in world rallying, with heroes such as the late, great Colin McCrae behind the wheel, it's no surprise that the boys from *Wheeler Dealers* would want to get their hands on one. A trawl through the classified adverts on the Internet found plenty of cars for sale, but there was just one problem – Mike had a budget of just £4,000 to buy his Impreza, and that made things a little more difficult. But there was to be a slice of luck as he finally tracked down a car for sale at a dealer, a trade-in that was for sale for a fiver under budget. It was a good-looking example too, in very original condition, with no signs of accident damage or modifications and with just two owners and 80,000 miles on the clock. It also benefitted from bodywork and an interior that were in excellent condition, so no work would be needed there. But was it too good to be true?

Well, naturally there were a few things that would need fixing, as Mike discovered on the test drive, but a bit of haggling saw him pay just £3,250 for this rallying legend.

Jobs to be tackled

The most obvious problems revealed on the test drive were a clutch that was slipping and clearly past its best, so that would need replacing. There was also a nasty judder from the brakes. Neither issue was desirable on a car like this, so they would have to be sorted, while signs of corrosion on the rear exhaust box meant that would need sorting too. Mike, though, had other plans for the WRX. It wasn't exactly lacking in power to begin with, but he wanted to add a bit more with some subtle upgrades, and improve the brakes to handle the extra go. The finishing touch would be some special body decals to add a unique *Wheeler Dealers* flavour. And all without breaking the bank. Could they do it? Of course they could.

Heading back to the workshop with the bargain Impreza saw MIke's concerns increase as the high clutch pedal and increasing difficulty in selecting gears caused him to wonder if he'd actually make it back to Edd without breaking down. And he was also beginning to wonder about how they could add value and make the sporting saloon stand out from all the others when the time came to sell, all on a small budget. But he needn't have worried, as he had the tall man standing by to work his magic.

First step in replacing the clutch was unbolting this bracing plate beneath the propshaft.

The propshaft flange bolts were next. Leave one in hand-tight to prevent it dropping down and causing injury.

With the centre bearing unbolted the propshaft could be withdrawn.

Replacing the clutch

The first steps

Changing the clutch on any car can be a tricky job, but the added complication of a four-wheel-drive system and tight packaging of the mechanicals meant there were plenty of parts that needed to be removed before the clutch itself could be replaced. And the cramped engine bay wasn't going to make the job any easier either.

With the Subaru up on the ramp, Edd's first job was to gain access to the major components, and that involved unbolting the protective shields beneath the engine and gearbox. A squirt of penetrating fluid on the bolts for these and the exhaust helped with removal, and with those out of the way the exhaust system and catalytic converter were next. This needed a methodical approach to avoid damage to these expensive parts. The exhaust downpipes were unbolted from the manifolds, and with the wiring for the oxygen sensors disconnected the supporting straps and hangers were removed and the entire exhaust system lifted clear. Fortunately it had been an easy task so far, but there is always the potential for exhaust fixings to be rusted in place, so Edd's advice is to take things slowly and be prepared to apply some heat to bolts and joints if they appear badly corroded. The last thing you want is for studs or bolts to shear – removal could add hours to an already long job, so a gentle approach can pay dividends.

The propshaft was next for removal. Edd began by undoing the six bolts that secured the bracing plate below the rear propshaft joint. With that out of the way he could undo the four bolts that secured the propshaft to the rear differential, leaving one in place just finger-tight to make sure that it didn't drop down unexpectedly and cause injury. Moving towards the front of the car, the centre prop bearing was unbolted and then the bolts attaching the prop to the gearbox, and with those undone the last rear bolt could be removed and the propshaft withdrawn.

The front driveshafts were next, which meant the front suspension would come in for attention. With both front wheels removed Edd could set about disconnecting the components that would enable the front wheel hubs to be moved outwards, an important job if there was to be

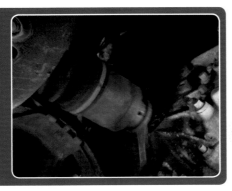

With the securing pin removed the driveshafts could be prised from the gearbox.

How much did it cost?

Car	£3,250
Performance parts	£405
Brakes and wheels	£850
Paint and graphics	£300
Engine re-mapping	£450
Total	*£5,255*

enough room to withdraw the driveshafts. The drop links between the suspension strut and anti-roll bar were unbolted and removed, and with the retaining nut undone the lower hub ball joint could be separated. Carefully tapping out the securing roll-pins allowed the driveshafts to be withdrawn from the gearbox, with the wheel hubs pulled outwards to give the necessary clearance.

It had been a lot of work so far, but Edd wasn't finished yet. Although the flat-four engine is relatively compact there are plenty of bulky ancillaries that can get in the way of jobs like these, so to further improve access the intercooler and associated inlet pipework both had to be removed. This was a matter of undoing securing bolts and clips, so not a difficult job, but since it was important not to damage anything a bit of care was needed. And as always, it was important to take notes or pictures to aid refitting.

The last bit of preparation was removing the

▼ The Impreza was a huge success in world rallying thanks to the exploits of drivers such as Colin McRae and Richard Burns (seen here). *(Subaru)*

Removing this plug gave access to the pin for the clutch release arm.

Using a transmission jack to support the engine before the next stage, gearbox removal.

pin for the clutch release arm. This involved a very particular process of which few people would be aware. It was a perfect example of the benefits of talking to experts before starting work. First off was unscrewing the Allen-head plug in the gearbox housing, and then winding in an M6-size bolt. With this in place the release arm pin could be withdrawn. All in all there had been plenty of stripping down to do so far but the job was progressing well, and it was time to move on to the next stage.

The Impreza's gearbox is a heavy item so Edd appreciated the extra pair of hands.

Removing and fitting of the new clutch

It was now time to separate the gearbox from the engine, and with the engine and gearbox supported by a transmission jack the securing bolts were removed (taking note of the sizes and positions of each bolt, as they can differ), and the gearbox carefully lowered. An extra pair of hands was useful here.

The clutch cover and pressure plate were secured to the flywheel with six bolts, and with these undone and the cover removed the clutch friction plate could be withdrawn. It was obviously badly worn, a comparison with the new part showing that the friction material was level with the securing rivets. It had been discovered just in time, as further use would almost certainly have caused costly damage to the flywheel. It would be replaced with an uprated part capable of handling up to 300bhp, which would allow for the performance modifications that were planned. In fact it's a handy tip for any owner thinking of boosting engine power in the future and an example of 'future-proofing' a car to avoid the need for further work.

It's taken a lot of time to get this far but the slipping clutch can finally be replaced.

The clutch is secured to the flywheel with a number of bolts, as shown here.

Buying one

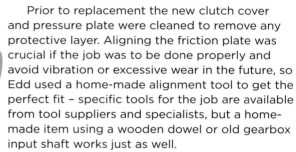

➔ **Accident damage is a real possibility so examine it carefully for signs of previous repairs, and make sure you get a history check. Rot isn't a particular issue but check the wings, door bottoms, sills and floorpan, just in case.**

➔ **The boxer engine is tough but needs meticulous maintenance. Oil leaks, head gasket failure and worn turbos are issues, while power upgrades are rife and affect longevity if not done properly.**

➔ **Listen for clunks and groans that indicate problems with the four-wheel-drive system. Power boosts put a strain on the gearbox and clutch and parts are costly, so don't ignore issues here.**

➔ **Interior trim was on the flimsy side so watch for wear and tear. The electrics shouldn't give problems, though, so just check that everything works.**

➔ **Imports are common and the model variations can be confusing, so it's best to speak to the owners' club or specialists so that you know what you're buying.**

Prior to replacement the new clutch cover and pressure plate were cleaned to remove any protective layer. Aligning the friction plate was crucial if the job was to be done properly and avoid vibration or excessive wear in the future, so Edd used a home-made alignment tool to get the perfect fit – specific tools for the job are available from tool suppliers and specialists, but a home-made item using a wooden dowel or old gearbox input shaft works just as well.

With the clutch cover bolted into place, all that was left was a few hours of labour to refit all of the components that had been removed. Everything went back together without a hitch, although, as Edd advises, it always pays to take plenty of notes or pictures

Fitting the new clutch assembly is straightforward. Edd used a home-made alignment tool, but you can buy them cheaply.

With all the components refitted it's just a case of replacing the engine undershield.

when disassembling complex parts, and to store components with their fixings to prevent any confusion or loss of important screws and

bolts. He had no trouble this time and the new clutch was all ready to handle the extra power that Mike had planned.

Upgrading the brakes and wheels

Testing the brakes and sourcing replacements

On the test drive Mike had noticed a judder under braking, the usual indicator of warped discs, so the first job for Edd was checking their condition. Using a dial gauge he checked the run-out of the front discs – as the disc turned the gauge would reveal how far out-of-true they were – and they were definitely warped, with almost half a millimetre of lateral movement on one disc. The brake calipers

The dial gauge shows that the front brake discs have had it, so an upgrade is on the cards.

The rusty brake calipers would go too but originals can be refurbished to save money.

Mike found these replacement brakes at a specialist. Sometimes bigger is just better!

were showing signs of corrosion too, so a whole new set-up was needed at the front. Fortunately, the benefit of upgrading a car like the Subaru is that there are often other higher performance variants in the range, so most models are all ready to accept later parts.

As always it was down to Mike to come up with the goods, so it was off to a Japanese performance car specialist to find something suitable for the project Impreza, and as usual he delivered in spades. A bigger set of discs was bought – now an impressive 330mm in diameter, compared to the 290mm original items – and matched with a set of huge four-piston, aluminium Brembo calipers. There certainly wouldn't be any problems in the stopping department, then. Mike wasn't finished yet though, as the larger brakes needed bigger wheels to match, so the alloys and tyres from an STI model (with a deeper offset) were snapped up, bringing the total spend to £1,050. A bit of classic wheeler dealering brought the price down to £850, Mike part-exchanging the original alloy wheels, which were in good condition.

Fitting the new brakes and wheels

Before fitting could begin, Edd's first task was to clean the replacement discs with brake cleaner to get rid of any accumulated grime or grease that would affect their operation. With that done, the flexible brake hoses were clamped, and then unscrewed at the caliper. The two bolts holding the brake caliper to the mounting bracket were undone, and the old calipers and discs were removed. It was then a simple job of bolting on the new parts – no modifications were needed, as the wheel hubs were all ready to accept the new parts – including the addition of new brake pads, which were included in the deal. Held in place by a spring plate and retaining pins at the top and bottom of the caliper, these got a dab of copper grease on the mounting points and the back of each pad. This would prevent them sticking in the caliper and prevent brake squeal, though care was needed to avoid getting grease on the friction surface. But replacing the pads was a simple job and one that could be considered a DIY task if you felt confident. With the system bled and a fill of fresh DOT4 fluid, the brakes were done and would be well up to the job of stopping the rapid Subaru.

Edd had done a great job as always and the stopping power was going to be much improved, but his advice is always to be careful when working on the braking system. If you're not sure about doing the work, it's far better to get an expert to do it for you.

The new wheels added a finishing touch, but as the original STI gold paint finish wasn't going to suit the project car they were sent off to be resprayed in satin black. They'd match the silver paintwork perfectly.

▼ Various alloy wheel designs were available, such as... these OZ items. *(Chris Rees)*

▼ ...or these fitted to the limited edition RB5 model, the RB referring to the late rally driver, Richard Burns. *(Chris Rees)*

With the brake hoses clamped Edd can get on with removing the old discs and calipers.

New brake pads were fitted, with a dab of copper grease on the mounting points to prevent sticking.

The brake work is almost done. They'll give the Impreza serious stopping power.

The new brakes meant bigger wheels, the second-hand items getting a coat of paint for a mean new look.

Performance upgrades

© Subaru

Ever since cars first arrived people have wanted to improve them in some way, making them go faster or handle better. And there are plenty of *Wheeler Dealers* projects where Mike and Edd have added value by doing just that. Here are a few things to consider:

- Before spending any money, think about the end result you're looking to achieve. Do you simply want to make the car faster, or improve usability by making it a better all-round driver?
- Talk to clubs and specialists about which modifications work best for your particular car. Chances are there is someone that has done the job before, and their experience will prove invaluable.

- There are plenty of small upgrades – such as better induction and exhausts systems – that can improve performance at a modest cost. ECU upgrades can do the same on more recent classics.
- Don't be tempted to go too far. Big power outputs can seem like a good idea, but they can ruin the car's driveability and reliability.
- Don't forget about other modifications to the running gear that may be needed to cope with the extra performance. You might need to consider upgrading the clutch, brakes and suspension if you've added substantially to the original power output.

Adding power

A new air filter and exhaust system

With an exciting ECU re-map planned, the boys wanted to be sure that the Impreza would benefit fully from the new power, so the car would get an upgraded air filter and exhaust system first.

Swapping the standard air filter element for a performance item would improve the engine's breathing, helping to get as much air into the cylinders as possible, and it was an easy job. Releasing the two clips on the air filter housing soon had the old paper element removed, and in its place went an uprated cotton gauze item that had also received a light coating of oil to help trap even more dust and dirt. Not only would the less restrictive design allow a better flow of air, but it was also washable, a quick clean every 50,000 miles or so keeping it at peak performance and saving money on replacements too. A bit of care was needed on refitting though – the new filter was slightly thicker than the original, so it was important for Edd to be sure that it was fitted correctly in the housing, and that the securing clips were fully engaged.

The exhaust system had already been removed for the clutch renewal so it was done separately on the show, and as Edd explained it was a relatively straightforward DIY task, just needing a basic toolkit. A spray of penetrating fluid on the various clamp bolts made removal easy, and with the mounting springs and hangers disconnected the old system could be lifted clear. The replacement was a good condition, second-hand big-bore system – 3in in diameter rather than around 2in for the original system – from another Impreza, so it fitted perfectly, and with the clamps firmly secured and mounting hangers refitted it was good to go.

Although it was now of a larger diameter –

Edd removes the old air filter ready for the new performance item.

▼ The crankshaft from an Impreza's boxer engine. It's strong enough to handle power increases but an upgrade may be needed if outputs get too high. *(Chris Rees)*

accentuating the wonderful off-beat thrum of the flat-four engine – it wouldn't necessarily boost power on its own, but combined with the freer-breathing air filter it would certainly make the most of the ECU work to come. And costing just £180, this was a budget-friendly way of improving the terrific Subaru.

The second-hand big bore exhaust will help make the most of the power upgrade and it's easy to fit.

The exhaust mountings and springs just need refitting and then it's time to find some more horsepower.

The ECU re-map

Despite Edd's awesome technical skills this wasn't a DIY task, so it was off to a performance specialist for the engine's electronic brain – the ECU – to be re-mapped and release a few extra horsepower. But his advice? Do your homework on the options available so you pick exactly the right sort of upgrade for your car – getting it wrong could be an expensive mistake and actually make things worse, so don't rush into things.

This was going to be the right choice for the Impreza, though. The first requirement was to find out how much power the engine was producing in its current form. So with the Impreza on a rolling road and the cooling fans in place, the motor was run up to peak revolutions and its outputs measured. And the initial results were slightly disappointing. A maximum reading of 206hp was actually down on the standard figure, although there was an explanation for this. It seemed that the new air filter and exhaust system were probably confusing the ECU a little, causing it to peg back the power at this stage, but Edd needn't have worried. With the laptop plugged into the car's diagnostic port, the specialist could study the standard ECU settings to see where adjustments could be made – being able to make better use of higher quality, super unleaded fuel, for example – and with a few clicks of the keys the new settings were programmed in.

Another session on the rolling road revealed the changes had been a success, the Impreza's turbocharged engine now delivering a much healthier 243.5hp – a very solid improvement, and one that would bring about definite gains in on-road performance. Those big new brakes were definitely going to be needed!

These Imprezas are great cars and just offer so much performance for the money, so basically I'm a bit of a fan. The main thing really is avoiding the abused ones that have been thrashed and any with massive power outputs that put a strain on all the mechanicals. Tuning them is really popular but some people go too far without doing other modifications, so it's asking for trouble. Although we gave ours a bit of a power boost it was pretty modest really, and we knew it wouldn't affect the reliability. This was also one of the first projects for the show that I bought from a dealer, and really I wanted to show that if you buy carefully you can still add value this way.

The other thing I remember from this one is the signed stripes that we put on. Both myself and Edd thought it would be a good idea, but it didn't go down well with all of the viewers. Judging by the feedback we had afterwards, it seems that opinion was split 50/50 and some people really hated them. I still think they looked good, though!

Adding some exterior style

With the mechanical work done the Impreza was in tip-top condition and ready for the road. But there was one last job that would put the finishing touches to this superb project – the addition of

Edd looks on anxiously as the power is measured using a rolling road.

He needn't have worried. This is a sound improvement on the original figure and will seriously improve performance.

some unique vinyl stripes, unique because they would include the signatures of Mike and Edd, a fantastic way of putting their stamp on another successful *Wheeler Dealers* project.

This was a two-person job, however, so Edd called in a specialist to help with applying them to the bodywork, and the first task was careful

measurement. The twin stripes would start at the front grille and head over the bonnet, the roof, and the boot lid and spoiler, so it was critical to get those measurements just right so the stripes were perfectly positioned along the centre of the bodywork. Once the positions were marked the panels were carefully cleaned with 'pre-paint' to

The styling stripes needed to be cut and carefully folded around items such as the bonnet scoop.

The finished car. It's a great new look and it goes and stops better than ever too.

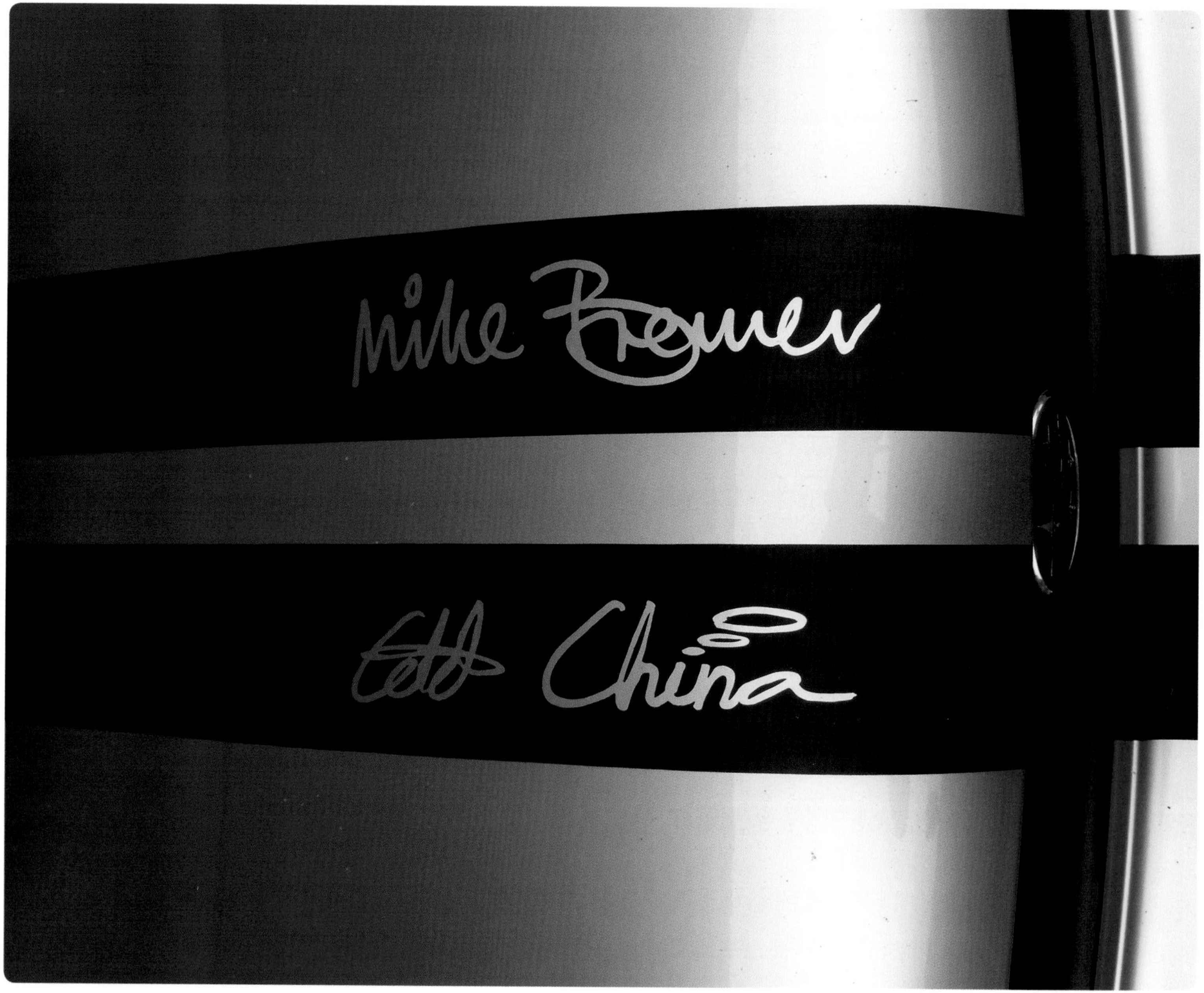
Mike Brewer
Edd China

After all that work the boys deserve to get their names on the car.

competing with plenty of other examples meant there wasn't a single call. These things happen, though. Dropping the price to £5,500 elicited more interest, and with some tough negotiating from Mike he shook hands with the new owner at £5,400.

ensure that grease or grime didn't prevent the decals adhering, and with that done the backing sheet could be removed and the stripes carefully laid in place. All that was left was to cut the stripes and very carefully fold them over any edges and creases in the bodywork (such as the intercooler intake on the bonnet) for a neat finished job.

Job done

The Subaru Impreza had arrived at the workshop with a few major problems, but with these fixed and some subtle improvements made it was worthy of the *Wheeler Dealers* stamp and ready to find a new owner. Which would actually turn out to be harder than expected. Mike had advertised the car on various mainstream websites for £6,000, but

Final test drive

With fantastic performance on offer the Subaru needed a special place for its test drive, which is how Mike and Edd found themselves at the Rockingham circuit in Northamptonshire. Donning crash helmets, and with Edd looking a little nervous, Mike took the wheel to put this rapid saloon through its paces on the fast straights and twisty corners of the track, and, just as expected, it performed superbly. The new brakes gave fantastic stopping power, but it was the uprated performance that Mike really wanted to sample, and he proved the worth of the modifications in a 0–60mph test. The car flew through the benchmark figure in an impressive 5.5 seconds.

Despite the four-wheel-drive system, working on the Subaru wasn't all that difficult, but it was one of the cars that perfectly illustrates the benefit of talking to experts, which is something that both of us would thoroughly recommend. In fact it's something we do a lot before tackling the projects – there is a huge amount of knowledge out there with owners' clubs and marque specialists, so it would be crazy not to make use of that. The particular job I'm thinking of here was changing the clutch, when I needed to remove the pin for the clutch release arm. Access to it was via a plug in the gearbox and without speaking to an expert first you'd have a real job finding and removing the pin correctly. It's so easy to waste time or, worse still, damage something by not doing the job properly, so it just makes sense to get proper advice first.

Amphicar

The classic car world is full of the quirky and unusual, but perhaps few vehicles are more quirky than this one. The Amphicar was made in Berlin, Germany, between 1961 and 1968 and in total just 3,878 were produced. Powered by a rear-mounted Triumph Herald engine that managed just 43hp, and drove through a four-speed manual gearbox for road use, this innovative machine could manage a top speed of 70mph, while on the water a two-speed transmission and twin nylon propellers were used to power it to just 7mph.

The vast majority of these cars would find their way to the US – a little over 3,000 examples, in fact – but it was this reliance on the American market that would be the Amphicar's undoing. Stricter regulations for 1968 effectively outlawed the car over the pond, and with sales collapsing production would finish that same year.

With fewer than 4,000 of these unusual vehicles produced, Mike was going to have his work cut out finding one for sale, and a search of the Internet revealed just two for sale in Europe. It was one of Edd's favourite cars, though – he'd been a fan of them since childhood – and, not wanting to let him down, Mike headed to America to track one down. Sure enough, he found this particular 1964 model for sale in Florida, with a price tag of $35,000. It was being sold by a restorer of these cars, and it looked OK on the surface. The front compartment was secured by locks on each side that were opened by a special key – an extra measure to ensure that the lid didn't open due to water pressure – and a look

Jobs to be tackled

Ever since Mike's test drive it had become obvious that the Amphicar was going to need a lot of work to get it back to its best – and, more importantly, if it was to fetch the highest price come sale time. There were numerous bodywork issues to tackle – some looking pretty serious – that would ultimately lead to a full respray. The bilge pump was going to need replacing, and there was the little matter of ensuring the Amphicar was going to pass the safety inspection that would allow it to take to the water. Would this prove to be one of the biggest jobs *Wheeler Dealers* had ever tackled? It was time to find out.

inside revealed a slightly scruffy but essentially solid-looking area. The engine bay looked fine too, with no obvious problems apparent with the little Triumph engine. But closer examination revealed a few problems, including signs of corrosion and some tired exterior trim and fittings.

However, ignoring thoughts of crocodiles Mike took to the water for one of the most fun test drives he'd ever had, in which he noticed that the cabin and front compartment were a bit damp. Not a good sign. It drove OK on the road, though, and there was some good news, because both the

hood and interior trim were in excellent condition. So Mike was happy to go back to the seller and try to do a deal, although he faced a tough challenge. Despite using all of his haggling skills the seller wouldn't budge on the price, so Mike had no choice but to pay the full asking price – a cool £21,000 at the time. But he was happy with the deal, and more importantly Edd would be thrilled to get his hands on the most unusual vehicle ever to grace the *Wheeler Dealers'* workshop.

Assessing the bodywork

With the Amphicar back in the UK and in the workshop, Edd's first job was going to be investigating the state of the bodywork, and what he found was somewhat alarming. With the car up on the ramp, the first area he checked was the floorpan beneath the driver's seat, and the sight of a disintegrating repair patch wasn't good news. Much closer investigation was going to be needed, so Edd set about removing the interior trim for a better look.

The seats simply unbolted, and with the carpets (which didn't really suit a car designed

Time to examine the state of the floor, and things didn't look good. Edd was in for some late nights...

The fibreglass patch that was partly to blame for the water leaks.

How much did it cost?

Car	£21,000
Shipping and travel	£2,500
Spare parts	£800
Stripping and respray	£5,500
Safety modifications and fees	£800
Total	**£30,600**

for the water!) and floor panels lifted away the full extent of the problem was revealed. The repair had been made using a fibre-glass patch – fine for a conventional boat, but not so good on a steel floor – and it was lifting away. Removing it all showed that some kind of rubber sealant had been employed to help keep water out, although the debris and leaves in the floor area showed this clearly hadn't worked. As well as the main hole there was serious corrosion around the sill, and at the junction of other panels and strengthening beams. It couldn't really have been any worse, and

Edd's Amphicar dream was beginning to turn into a nightmare.

Further checks underneath showed more evidence of past repairs around the front and rear of the 'hull', Edd using a small mallet and chisel to remove patches of filler to reveal dents, rust holes and, worse still, evidence of numerous previous bodges. Indeed, closer examination of the filler showed just how many layers had been added over

Chipping away the fibreglass revealed the full extent of the problem.

Some kind of rubber sealant had been applied to help keep the water out, but this was a real bodge.

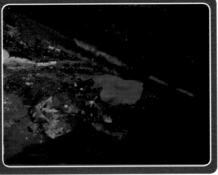

The rust that Edd was going to spend hours cutting out and replacing with fresh metal.

This shows the extent of the corrosion that Edd was facing. It's not a pretty sight.

With the trim and panels removed, Edd could get on with removing the paint.

the years. Oh, and there was also the matter of bubbling in the lower section of the nearside rear quarter panel. Judging by the way the paint had blistered it was clear that the metalwork was rotten beneath, but a more drastic method was needed to reveal the full extent of the bodywork issues.

Soda blasting

That method was soda blasting. More gentle than other methods such as sand blasting, it would allow Edd to remove old paint and filler and see

exactly where the damage was but without causing damage to healthy metalwork.

The first stage was to remove all of the exterior trim, so he began at the front by unbolting the bumper and removing the light bezels and light units. With the front compartment stripped of any internal trim – including the carpeted sections that would be replaced later – the next job was to carefully unbolt the doors, the front bonnet and the rear engine compartment cover. The remainder of the exterior trim was removed and stored, and finally he could get started.

As Edd himself explained, soda blasting was a messy and laborious task, so a good few hours had to be allowed to do the job properly – it would actually take two days to do the whole car – but it was very effective, and a blaster could be hired for around £300. Starting with the rear quarter panel, the expected filler and holes were found in the lower section, although the rest of the panel looked in good condition. Most of the other panels got the same treatment, taking them back to bare metal, and Edd soon found plenty more filler – up to half an inch thick in places – as well as the remains of

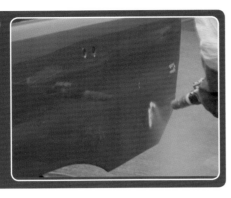

Soda-blasting was effective but time-consuming, but it was gentle on the metalwork.

The rotten rear quarter panel is revealed, and would require more of Edd's body repair skills.

expanding foam. Neither of which would have been useful in keeping the Amphicar afloat. All in all there was plenty of evidence of poor previous repairs, the bodywork in a much poorer state than either Mike or Edd had bargained for!

Repairing the rear quarter panel

With the soda blasting finished and the car back in the workshop, the next job would be repairing that rotten rear panel. With eye and ear protection donned, Edd used a grinder to cut away the lower section of the panel, taking care to remove only the rusty section until solid metal was reached. As always with this sort of job it was important not to remove more metal than necessary, to avoid making repairs bigger than they need to be. Unfortunately the panel behind was also rotten, so that was cut out too. The dreaded expanding foam that he found clearly just acted as a moisture trap, causing the panel to rust from the inside out.

MIG welding a new section in place. It was done carefully to avoid distorting the surrounding metal.

Cutting fresh steel to replace the rot. As always, careful measurement is needed to avoid mistakes.

The new rear quarter panel is tacked into place with time allowed between each weld to avoid heat damage.

Folded seams helped secure the panels to each other. A careful approach is needed to ensure the correct panel fit.

With a new inner panel spot-welded into place, Edd could get on with making a repair section from sheet steel, using the old panel as a template. This stage needed care if the panel was to fit correctly, and it was important to allow extra metal around the edge for the folds and seams needed to refit it (the seams effectively folded around adjacent panels to help fix them in place). Getting those seams right required a careful approach – it's never worth trying to rush these jobs – so Edd used a small metal press to make half folds first. Back on the bench, he could use another piece of metal to act as a guide and then use a small panel-beating hammer to gently tap the folds over to just the right thickness.

Happy with the shape of the repair section and the trial fit to the car, it was time to tack it into position, allowing time between each weld to prevent heat distortion. With the new panel in place and the rot eliminated, all that was left was to weld up and then fill the holes in the upper section of the wing that had been left by incorrectly located bilge exits. Now it was time to tackle that rotten floor.

Repairing the floor

This was beginning to look like the biggest bodywork repair job that Edd had ever taken on, and this next stage was going to need a lot of patience if it was to be done properly.

With the protective gear on, the first step was careful use of the grinder to remove the rotten floor panel and the triangular strengthening section. And again it was a case of checking and measuring before cutting, to ensure all of the rot was removed without taking away too much of the surrounding solid metal. The less that needs to be replaced the better in these situations. Once done, a new floor section was cut from fresh steel and the edges shaped to ensure it would neatly butt-up against the existing metalwork. With the repair section held in place using magnets, it was tack-welded into position. It was important to get the shape and position of the triangulating section absolutely right, as not only would it add crucial extra strength to the floor but it also allowed for the flow of any water that might leak into the cabin, so a paper template was used to cut the exact shape from sheet steel.

With the template folded into shape, the next step was making the holes that would save weight as well as allowing for that flow of water should the

Using a paper template will help to get the shape of the strengthening section spot-on.

Time to cut out the new section, after accurate measurement of course.

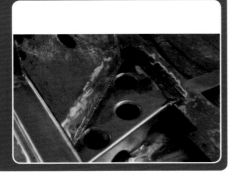

All that hard work paid off. The new section fits perfectly and the rust repairs are almost finished.

Buying one

➔ **Corrosion is a major issue, so examine every panel and the floor thoroughly. A full restoration will swallow plenty of cash so get it inspected by a specialist.**

➔ **It's a car that will need regular maintenance to give its best so ensure you're happy with the commitment required. A neglected one will be a money pit.**

➔ **The Triumph Herald engine is a tough unit and easy to rebuild, so just check for signs of fluid leaks, excessive exhaust smoke and lack of regular servicing.**

➔ **The Amphicar contains plenty of unique parts so cost and availability can be an issue. Make sure exterior and interior trim parts are present and correct.**

➔ **Rarity keeps values high and originality is key, so speak to an expert before taking the plunge. It's vital to avoid bodged and incomplete restorations.**

worst happen. For this Edd used a special tool – costing £120 and sourced online – that would both cut the hole to the required size and form the vital swaged edge to each opening, and it was a task that he would spend a lot of time on as this certainly wasn't the moment to rush such a crucial stage of the repair. Unfortunately it wasn't possible to form exactly the right size of aperture in the new section – the tool needed was an unusual size – but it was very close, and Edd had given plenty of thought to the design, with a slight modification actually improving the potential water flow. As always, some

practice was advised before tackling the job for real, a good tip of course for any major bodywork repairs. Once happy that the section fitted perfectly, it was welded into place, and the new floor was finally finished.

It had taken a huge number of hours both on and off camera to remove all of the rot and let in fresh metal, but it was a job that would have cost thousands of pounds at a specialist, so well worth tackling yourself if you feel confident enough.

The Amphicar was finally ready for the spray booth, and with a new bonnet fitted – the original

Importing a classic

- Unless you are certain of a car's provenance and condition, view it for yourself. Don't rely on pictures or owner descriptions.

- Ensure you understand the costs involved, including shipping, taxes and any storage charges if you can't collect the car immediately after landing.

- Know the legislation. Imports must be registered via the 'Notification of Vehicle Arrivals' (NOVA) form, and to avoid fines this must be done within 14 days of the car arriving. You can't apply for registration or an MOT certificate until the NOVA form is processed.

- Find a reputable agent to handle the paperwork. The bureaucracy involved can be a minefield and a reliable agent will understand local rules and regulations and provide peace of mind.

- Think about the best method of transporting your new classic. If it's road legal you could drive it back, but transporting by sea or air are more likely. Investigate the costs and be sure the shipping company will handle your treasured car with care.

- If you've travelled to see the car, take plenty of pictures before it's shipped. Parts can be pilfered from old or valuable cars during the journey, so you'll want to have proof of its condition.

- Make sure you've arranged transportation from the landing place in the UK to your home or workshop. It's recommend you don't drive the vehicle away, so you will probably need a trailer.

Back from the paint shop and looking fantastic, but there's still plenty of work to do as you can see.

was so full of filler that it was beyond repair – the bodywork was prepared and primed ready for fresh paint to be applied. The boys had chosen to respray it in the original Regatta Red, and while at £4,000 the job hadn't been cheap, it looked fantastic.

With all the exterior trim refitted and panels such as the doors and engine cover bolted back on, Edd was almost ready to tackle the rest of the work. However, this stage wouldn't be completely trouble-free, as it would take a few hours to get the fit of the doors just right. There was a unique latching arrangement that ensured the seals would remain watertight – pretty vital on a car like this – and it proved a tricky task to get everything correctly aligned. But as the test drive proved, Edd's perseverance had paid off.

Replacing the bilge pump

Like most boats, the Amphicar was fitted with a bilge pump so that any water that did find its way in could be safely pumped out. It was located beneath the rear seat, but further investigation revealed an arrangement that was past its best. Firstly the switch that acted as a float and activated the pump hadn't been secured properly, and the wiring looked none too good either. It wasn't even an original part as these are especially expensive, so with the securing screw undone from underneath the car and the pipework disconnected Edd could remove it and set about some dismantling and testing. It was theoretically rated to shift 1,500 gallons of water per hour, but testing it using some crates of water it didn't appear all that efficient, and once stripped down it was clear that there was wear to the impellor vanes and pump casing. There was nothing

The old bilge pump was past it, so Edd sourced a replacement to help keep the Amphicar from sinking.

The mounting bracket for the new bilge pump needs to be fitted first.

The new activating switch for the pump has been properly secured this time, and works perfectly.

The handmade paddles were a lovely touch, and Mike got involved in making them too.

for it but to source a new kit from a boat shop, Edd choosing a higher-rated item for maximum efficiency.

Fitting the new pump would prove relatively straightforward. He'd decided to mount the unit in the centre of the chassis where it would be able to collect the most water, so the first step was drilling holes in the floorpan to mount the pump bracket – making sure, of course, that there were no components or obstructions underneath. With the bracket screwed securely into position, the various hoses could be attached to the pump using jubilee clips, and the pump clipped into the bracket. Edd then welded a couple of studs to the floor so the activating switch could be held in place with nuts, and the three holes left in the floor panel by the previous pump were welded up. Although not shown, a manual override switch was also fitted, just in case the item supplied with the kit failed to activate – as such an important item it was always going to be better to have the pump running more rather than less!

With the wiring for the new pump connected all that was left to do was to route the bilge's outlet hose through the engine bay to the correct outlet hole in the offside of the rear panel. Edd sourced a new chrome finisher to replace the plastic item that had been fitted originally, although he left the latter in the glovebox in case the new owner wanted to retain the standard appearance. It was easy to fit, just fed through from the exterior of the panel and secured on the inside with a washer and nut.

Some finishing touches

While Edd was busy in the workshop Mike had been on the road, visiting a traditional boatyard to source a couple of items that would help add a final flourish to the Amphicar – a pair of delightful, handmade paddles. Costing just £80 each, they were made from three blocks of spruce wood that were glued together, cut and shaped, then planed and sanded for the perfect shape and finish. With two coats of marine varnish applied, and a signwriter adding special *Wheeler Dealers* logos (with a bit of help from Mike), they would be perfect additions to the finished project.

There was still more work to be done, though. The next task was refitting the seats and interior trim. The rather strange carpeted panels in the front luggage compartment were discarded and replaced by new, handmade marine-quality boards that added £200 to the cost. The fuel tank was ready to be refitted into the front compartment, but first it would need to be coated in waterproof sealant to ensure it met all of the required safety regulations.

Obtaining a safety certificate

Getting this vital piece of paper was next on the list, and it was a crucial job if the car was going to be allowed in the water. The rules had changed a lot since the Amphicar was built, so before the visit of the boat safety examiner, Edd had plenty to do to get the car ready for inspection.

The first stage was to swap the fuel hoses for marine-specification items, and these were covered in a protective plastic sheath. To prevent the build-up of fuel vapour in the front compartment an external fuel filler was required, which Edd located in the offside scuttle panel just below the windscreen. An external breather was also needed that contained a gauze filter to prevent water ingress. This was sited adjacent to the new fuel filler. Both would require drilling suitable holes in the bodywork – a shame in Edd's view, as it spoiled

The carpeted panels are gone and replaced by these lovely new boards. Handmade, they cost £200.

Edd wrestles with the refurbished fuel tank, but it's actually quite easy to fit.

Mods included an external fuel filler and breather, as shown here. A gauze filter helps prevent water ingress.

The fuel tank was modified with new fittings so that it met current regulations.

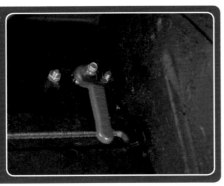

Another safety modification, this is the fuel shut-off valve that Edd located beneath the dashboard.

An electrical cut-off switch was also required. It was easy to wire in and mounted within easy reach.

the originality – but there was little choice if UK regulations were to be met.

More work was needed on the fuel tank itself. With the tank cleared of any remaining vapour – a vital safety point, and work perhaps best left to a specialist – the original fuel inlet and outlet apertures were welded up and new holes made for the revised filler and vent pipes. Also required for certification was a fuel shut-off valve in the cabin, so Edd located this on the offside of the front bulkhead, and an electrical master switch needed fitting. To ensure it was within easy reach of the driver, he chose to position this just below the rear seat squabs, and it was a quick job to bolt it into position and wire it in to the car's electrical system.

With the correct warning stickers applied to indicate the location of the fuel and electrical switches the work was almost finished. All that was left was to clip a fire extinguisher in place below the dashboard and fit an approved waterproof casing around the battery. All of the hard work paid off, though, and the examiner was more than happy to issue the safety certificate. The Amphicar was ready to take to the water!

I have to say that at first I wasn't very keen on doing an Amphicar on the show. I'd never really rated it and there was a lot of debate about it, but in the end Edd won! But after taking the test drive I knew I'd completely misunderstood this one. As soon as I got in the water I realised I absolutely loved it – it was just so much fun to be in and I was really keen to do the deal. The problem was how few there were to buy with the budget we had, and I knew as I was buying this one that it was going to need a massive amount of work. The bodywork was really poor, but it was still a shock when we uncovered the real extent of the problems. However, even after all that I'd definitely recommend them – find a good one and you'll absolutely love it.

The finishing touches, and the Amphicar was done. With the safety certificate signed, it was ready for the water!

A waterproof battery cover would help the Amphicar gain that all-important safety certificate.

Unfortunately, however, it wouldn't all be plain sailing. Mike and Edd couldn't wait to get the car into the river, and although all went well at first a loss of drive resulted in a tow back to the river bank and a return to the workshop for some more fettling. Thanks to the somewhat unique mechanicals it would be a week and quite a few hours of work before Edd had sorted the problem, replacing a broken needle roller bearing on the gearbox's first motion shaft. Previous water ingress and corrosion had almost certainly led to the part's failure and the gearbox and transfer box would need to be stripped down to reach it, but apart from the job being somewhat oily and messy it wasn't too difficult. With this £35 part replaced – luckily the parts supply for these vehicles is still very good – the Amphicar was finally finished and ready to find a new owner.

Job done

It had been a simply huge amount of work, with far more extensive body repairs needed than either of the boys envisaged, but all of the effort had paid off. The Amphicar looked absolutely terrific, and while it had been a big project for *Wheeler Dealers*,

the rewards would be equally large. It sold for a whopping £35,200!

Final test drive

With the Amphicar finished Edd was keen to give it a really good test, even going so far as to consider taking it across the Channel. And if that was a bit ambitious there was always the Solent and a trip to the Isle of Wight. But in the end thoughts of salt water attacking the lovely new bodywork called for a revised plan, which is how the boys found themselves bobbing around on the Thames in the shadow of Windsor Castle. Even that would prove a slight challenge, though, as recent flooding in the UK had left river levels high, and with the water flowing fast there were rescue crews on standby just in case. But after a champagne launch, and with both of them looking suitably nautical, Edd guided the Amphicar down the slipway and into the water, where it performed superbly. Until, that is, the mechanical problem with the gearbox intervened – but luckily rescue was at hand. It wasn't the ending they'd planned, but they had proved that the restoration had been a success and the Amphicar was now ready to hit the waterways.

I knew Mike wasn't at all keen on the Amphicar but I'd wanted to get one on the show for years, so it was a real push to get everyone to agree. And I'm happy to say I won that one. Mike's right, though, this one was in a really bad way and the state of the bodywork was a real shock – everywhere you looked there were signs of rust, damage, and previous bodges where people had just put filler on top of filler. It was a disaster area and took a full two days of soda-blasting to get it to a stage where I could start repairing it. I'm really happy with the way it turned out, though, and it definitely made all the hours we both put in worth it. It looked awesome when it was finished, and it's still one of my favourite classics!

Willys MB Jeep

If any vehicle deserves to be called an icon it's probably this one. The word 'jeep' has now entered into common usage, but it all started way back in 1940 when the American military laid out plans for a cheap, tough, go-anywhere vehicle. It arrived in 1941 based on a design by the American Bantam Car Company, and around 650,000 were made in total with production split between Willys Overland Motors and Ford. Packed with clever touches such as hinged headlamps that could illuminate the engine bay and holders for tools and weapons, it was truly a legend of the battlefield.

Of course, it has also played a starring role in many a war film, and with Mike a fan of the genre he was more than happy to head to the US to secure *Wheeler Dealers* their very own piece of military history. With $10,000 to spend it was the proper MB that he wanted, and after a search online he found one that looked ideal, apart from the fact that it was $5,000 over budget. But it was just the type he wanted – a 1945 model fitted with the classic flat-head L-type four-cylinder engine, boasting a handy 60bhp and lots of original features. It was in sound condition too – he'd checked to ensure the chassis wasn't rusty and that the engine ran OK – but it wasn't without problems, though these were nothing that technical supremo Edd couldn't solve. So using those famous bargaining skills Mike secured the MB for $13,000, or just £8,000.

Jobs to be tackled

While the bodywork was essentially solid – important on a vehicle like this – Mike had spotted a problem with the load-bay floor. It looked buckled, and repairs had been bodged in the past, so that would need sorting. He'd also experienced problems on the test drive, the gearbox being reluctant to engage third gear, and there were some cosmetic jobs to tackle. This restoration was going to be all about getting the details spot-on, so the incorrectly mounted jerrycan holder would need to be tackled and the tatty seat cushions replaced. As always, there was plenty for Edd to do.

The bodged floor panel would have to be replaced, and it was going to be a big job for poor old Edd.

Separating the body from the chassis meant plenty of parts to remove, starting with the bonnet.

The windscreen was next, but the simple construction meant it was easily unbolted.

Removing the inner wing was the next job.

Replacing the floor

Assessing the problem, and preparation

With the jeep safely delivered to the workshop Edd could set about assessing that buckled floor, and it was clear that replacement wouldn't be a quick job. It appeared that at some point the bolts securing the floor panel to the chassis had pulled through their mounting holes, and rather than fix it properly a previous owner had fitted large washers in the form of metal discs to keep things in place. Cosmetically, it looked poor, and with buyers of these vehicles sticklers for perfection and originality the whole panel would have to be replaced. And while it wasn't shown on screen, closer investigation in the workshop had revealed corrosion around the floor area – the reason for those poor original repairs – that would need to be fixed first.

Gaining proper access to the panel was the next challenge, and it was clear that the entire rear section of bodywork would have to be removed from the chassis; and with plenty of parts to remove, Edd advised allowing at least a day for a job like this. Thankfully the Jeep's simple construction meant a fairly simple toolkit would suffice.

The first task was unbolting the bonnet and windscreen frame. Then it was the turn of the fuel tank, which was mounted beneath the driver's seat. With the fuel pipes disconnected, the unit simply unbolted from the floor. Next it was time to locate and disconnect any wires and pipes between chassis and body – taking care to label them to aid reassembly – and then unbolt the nearside inner wing.

With that out of the way the joint between the steering column and steering box was unbolted, the steering wheel removed, the column clamp beneath the dashboard undone and the column itself withdrawn. The front and rear seats were easy to unbolt and they'd be put aside for future attention to the cushions. Locating all of the bolts that secured the body to the chassis was next, and after a squirt of penetrating fluid they came undone easily and were carefully stored to prevent any confusion later. After a final check to ensure that everything had been disconnected, the body was carefully lifted clear using the ramp, and the rolling chassis wheeled safely out of the way.

The steering column would need to come out, so off came that sturdy metal steering wheel.

Edd used the ramp to carefully lift the body from the chassis, ensuring nothing was left connected.

How much did it cost?

Car	£8,000
Shipping	£2,000
Body panel	£130
Gearbox and spares	£732
Total	*£10,862*

Removing the floor panel

A bit of preparation was needed before Edd could tackle removal. There were various components and brackets to be removed for access, including the footrests and jerrycan holder, and that lovely original dashboard was covered with a heavy cloth to prevent any damage to the instruments.

Wearing protective goggles and ear defenders

▼ The Jeep's simple engineering was designed to be easy to fix. And no, that's not a young Mike and Edd tackling this one! *(Warehouse Collection)*

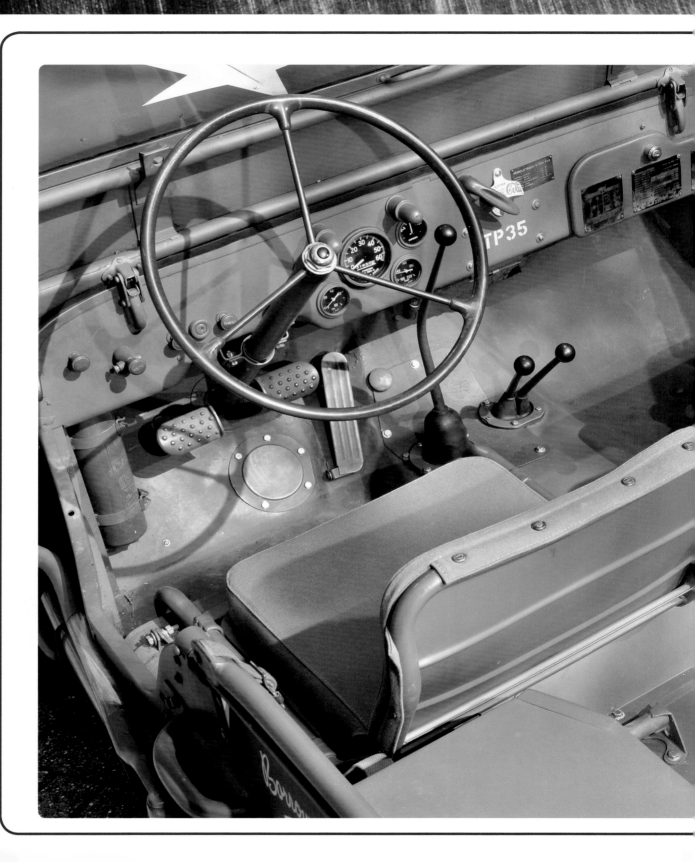

Edd could then set to work with the grinder, removing the paint to expose the original spot welds that attached the floor panel to the rest of the bodywork. Drilling out each weld was the first step, and here he used a special drill bit designed so that you can drill through the weld and top layer of metal only, rather than making a hole right through the panels. It was a fiddly and time consuming job but worth taking the time to get right on such an historic vehicle. Once again it showed the benefit of using the right tool for the job to avoid making extra work later.

Next a cutting disc was used to cut around the seams of the panel, making sure not to damage surrounding metalwork, and then it was time to separate the old floor section from the rest of the bodywork, again taking plenty of time just in case a weld had been missed somewhere. The seams and edges could then be cleaned up ready for the panel that Mike had obtained from the US.

The job had taken plenty of hours so far, and unseen on the show was the number of times that the bodywork had to be rotated in order to reach all of the numerous welds and seams. A lot of effort behind the scenes then, but with the aim of making

Drilling out the old spot welds was the first task, as these secured the floor panel to the body.

The seams of the old floor could be cut through but care was needed to prevent damage to surrounding metal.

A coat of conductive primer on the seams and edges readied the body for welding in the new floor panel.

Where the seams were inaccessible, plug welding was the best method of securing the panel.

Spot welding was used for the remaining areas, an authentic method used when the Jeep was new.

With the welds ground back, the finish was perfect and another good repair job had been completed.

the repair as close to the original specification as possible – this sort of attention to detail really counts with a car like the Jeep, and Edd was determined to retain as much of its originality as possible. So it was time and effort well spent.

The job was progressing well and test-fitting the new panel was the next stage. Once Edd was happy that it would fit properly – it's important to check first, as you can't always be certain that any replacement panel will fit as intended, and some adjustment may be needed – he proceeded to drill the holes in the seams that would be used for the plug welds (the original construction used spot welds throughout, but access was too difficult). With any remaining paint ground away – it would affect the quality of the welds – Edd decided that a mixture of plug and spot welds would be the best way to secure the floor panel. Not only would it leave the finished job looking as authentic and as close to the original build process as possible, but such careful assembly would ensure that he hadn't created any rust traps for the future.

Fitting the new panel

The first step, though, was to treat the seams of the new panel with special pre-welding primer, conductive paint that was specific for the job and would help prevent future corrosion. With the appropriate safety gear on and the panel clamped in position the front edge of the panel was carefully plug-welded – a job that needed patience, as time was allowed between each weld to prevent heat distortion damaging the panel. With those done, a spot welder was used to join the rest of the seams. Then, with the finished welds ground smooth and a small amount of filler applied for the perfect finish, the new panel was ready for painting.

Applying the paint

As always this was a job to be approached methodically if the perfect finish was to be obtained, so preparation would be needed. The panel was carefully rubbed down for a nice smooth surface and then pre-paint was used to remove any contaminants that would prevent the fresh paint adhering. A coat of etch primer was next – this would provide a 'key' for the paint – and then Edd had a decision to make. Applying a layer of stone-chip paint wouldn't be original of course, but it would add extra protection to

The bottom of the panel would get a coat of classic green paint, but not before a light stone-chip had been applied.

The final coat. Painting by hand was more authentic than a spray booth.

the finished job, and after a bit of thought it was decided that the latter was more important in this case, so a light stone-chip went on followed by a coat of primer.

With the correct colour of paint obtained from the States, Edd also decided that applying it by hand from an aerosol can would be more authentic than using a spray booth. So with the preparation complete, the new paint was applied evenly to the underside of the panel – the inside would be painted once the jerrycan holder had been repositioned, to prevent damaging the new paint with swarf. And with that last stage completed the Jeep's bodywork was in excellent shape once more.

Fitting a new gearbox

With the body separated from the chassis – a good reason to plan any renovation work in advance so you don't end up having to disassemble components more than once – this was the perfect time to tackle replacement of the duff gearbox. The US is a great place to source replacement parts for these cars, so while Mike was there he took the opportunity to do some shopping. New gearboxes

Buying one

→ Rust in the panels and floor are the main bodywork issues, so it needs a thorough examination. Thanks to the simple construction repairs are reasonably straightforward.

→ Make sure you check the chassis for rust, especially at the rear (oil leaks often protect the front). Damage from accidents or off-roading are possible too and can distort the chassis.

→ Originality is key, so look for a car with period features such as tools, fuel cans and the like. Sourcing them isn't too difficult but it's a good haggling point if they're missing.

→ There's a good parts supply – especially in the US – but there are lots of reproduction parts around that vary in quality. It's worth doing your homework before buying.

→ The interior couldn't be simpler and all the parts are available for refurbishment. 6V electrics were used originally, but converting to a 12V arrangement is a sensible modification.

Here's the replacement gearbox Mike had sourced from America. They are rare items so it was a lucky find.

A simple split-pin connected the clutch arm, making removal a quick job.

The magnetic gearbox drain plug had collected a lot of swarf. Things weren't well with the old 'box.

aren't available so a rebuilt one was obtained from a specialist, the correct Warner T84J three-speed unit. But there was plenty of work to do before the new unit could be fitted, so it was time for Edd to get cracking.

The boys only had instructions for tackling the job with the body in place, so a bit of thought was needed before getting started; but as Edd would tell you, it was certainly easier with the bodywork removed. The first task, then, was removing the split-pin and disconnecting the clutch lever from the 'box. To make the job a little easier he then drained the oil from the old unit, the metal filings clinging to the magnetic drain plug a clear sign that all wasn't well with the gearbox's internals.

Unbolting the two prop shaft joints and the bell housing came next, and then Edd needed to remove the gear cluster that coupled the gearbox shaft to the transfer box, the part that distributed drive to all four wheels. The cover plate was removed first – secured with five bolts – and, with the split-pin removed and the securing bolt undone, the gear cluster was withdrawn and the transfer box itself unbolted. And with the mating

The propshaft was easily unbolted, but make sure you keep any fixings safe for refitting.

This gear cluster coupled the gearbox and transfer box and needed to be removed.

Careful cleaning of the transfer box joints would avoid any oil leaks when everything had been refitted.

With just a few bolts undone, the heavy old gearbox could be withdrawn.

surfaces on the two units cleaned to aid refitting it was on with the rest of the job.

With the gear lever removed, the inspection plate on the gearbox housing was unbolted to allow access to the clutch release arm and release bearing. Then, with the release arm disconnected and the bolts between engine and gearbox undone, the unit was withdrawn from the chassis. It was almost time for installation, but first the new 'box got a coat of green paint – not strictly necessary, as it would be hidden from view, but this project was all about originality. With the clutch release arm swapped over and the new unit bolted back to the engine, the next step would be reconnecting the gear and transfer boxes, for which some care was needed.

As always it was important to take a methodical approach to jobs like these if mistakes were to be avoided, and the first stage was to carefully remove the wooden plate attached to the end of the gearbox – it was there to prevent disturbance to the gearbox's output shaft, as this would result in internal components becoming displaced, which was definitely not desirable. With the plate removed it was time to apply the special sealant to the joint faces of both units, and since the gearbox rebuilder recommended the use of 'Toyota FIPG103' sealant that, of course, was what Edd used.

The job was nearly finished, and with the gear and transfer boxes bolted back together it was just a case of refitting the transfer gear cluster removed earlier – ensuring the securing bolt was tightened to the correct torque, and with a new split-pin fitted

◄ Welcome to the Wheeler Dealers keep-fit plan! Apparently Mike did suggest using this method in the workshop although it seems that Edd prefers his ramp! *(Warehouse Collection)*

You don't want to spoil the authenticity so the new gearbox gets the same green paint as the rest of the Jeep.

Fitting the clutch release arm to the new 'box as Edd gets on with reassembling the transmission.

You can see the wooden plate on the new gearbox. It kept internal components in place, so care was needed on removal.

Special sealant was applied between the gearbox and transfer box, as recommended by the supplier in America.

One last job on the bodywork – drilling the holes in the new floor so it can be bolted to the chassis.

and the cover plate refitted; reconnecting the clutch lever (operating it by hand to check it worked OK); and filling the gearbox with the correct EP80 oil. The Jeep's gear change was sorted, and Edd was almost ready to move on to tackling the cosmetic issues.

I've been a fan of the WW2 Jeep for years so I was really pleased to finally get one on the show. I had great fun buying it as well, and the guy I bought it from turned out to be an absolute star – he's still a really great friend of mine and has helped us out a lot since, when we've bought cars from the US. Our one had some terrific original features and I was determined to protect that originality, as it's what these cars are all about. And it's one we both had to get exactly right, as we'd already decided to take the finished project to a military re-enactment event; so the pressure was on to make sure every detail was perfect. Both of us loved taking part in the event as well, although we did get a few complaints afterwards about the uniforms we were wearing! The good news with Jeeps is that parts are plentiful so it's a really easy classic to keep on the road, and it's also an easy car to sell. As soon as it was finished I had a queue of people waiting to buy it, so you can't really go wrong.

Refitting the bodywork to the chassis

With the new floor section and gearbox in place, Edd budgeted a day to get the bodywork fitted back on to the chassis. As he advised, it was worth assessing the condition of any fixings as they were removed, as new ones might be needed on reassembly. But before the two parts could be reunited, holes needed to be drilled in the new floor section to accept the chassis mounting bolts. Edd drilled from beneath the Jeep, using the original bolt holes as a guide and making sure to add a dab of paint to any bare metal to prevent future corrosion. The bolts were then fitted from the top and secured by nuts underneath. With that done it was a simple job replacing all of the parts removed previously, such as the fuel tank, seats, steering column and front wing – the simple engineering involved presenting few problems.

Repositioning the jerrycan holder

Buyers of vehicles like these want them to be accurate in every detail, which meant that items like the jerrycan holder needed to be positioned just as they would have been when the Jeep left the factory. This was tackled before the bodywork was refitted to the chassis. Edd was determined to get details like these as perfect as he could, and as he didn't have any exact measurements he spent plenty of time studying period pictures to establish the correct position, which was on the nearside of the rear panel adjacent to the spare wheel (it had previously been mounted behind the front seats).

▶ If it's good enough to raise a smile from allied D-Day commanders Dwight D. Eisenhower (front passenger) and General Omar N. Bradley (rear)... *(Warehouse Collection)*

Edd took his time getting the position of the jerrycan holder just right, referring to period photographs for help.

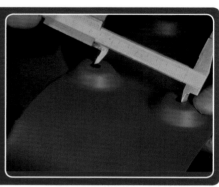

Careful measurement was needed before the mounting holes could be drilled in the rear panel.

Once happy with the position, it was time to drill the panel where the jerrycan holder would be bolted.

WILLYS TRUCK

¼ TON 4 x 4
MODEL MB

★ ★ ★

INSTRUCTIONS

FOR

UNPACKING & ASSEMBLY

OF BOXED

VEHICLE

★ ★ ★

MKD (Medium Knock-down) 148 Cubic Feet

WILLYS-OVERLAND MOTORS, INC.
TOLEDO, OHIO, U. S. A.

▲ "Okay Mike, where have you hidden the instructions…" These could have come in handy for poor old Edd as he tackled all those jobs. *(Warehouse Collection)*

Moving it wouldn't be entirely trouble-free, as he needed to avoid drilling through the strengthening bars on the rear of the panel while at the same time ensuring the holder was mounted securely. As always it was going to be a case of measure twice, cut once (or in this case drill once), so Edd took plenty of time getting the position just right, making adjustments until he was completely happy. Then he marked the bodywork and started drilling from the inside of the panel. A dab of paint around the edges of the holes would prevent corrosion setting in, and the holder was secured in place with four bolts. With the jerrycan slotted in, it was another delightful period feature to impress a buyer.

The final jobs

Mike's shopping trip in America had netted some more period parts that would add desirability to the finished Jeep, vital if the boys were to get the best price when the time came to sell, so these were fitted next. The wonderfully original first-aid kit just clipped into position beneath the dashboard, and the wiper linkage – manually operated, with not a motor in sight – that Mike had sourced was bolted to

Mike had also bought a few tasty extras for the Jeep, including these manually operated wipers.

A genuine first-aid kit adds the finishing touch. Luckily it wasn't needed during the project!

the top of the windscreen frame. Then it was time to get rid of the tatty seat covers that were letting the car down and screw new items into place.

Job done

The project was finished, and Mike and Edd had pulled it off again, turning this solid but slightly unloved wartime classic into a fantastic example that would bear any scrutiny. All that was left was for Mike to sell the Jeep, a car that owed them a substantial £10,800, but there was no need to worry. They'd done a fantastic job as always and the new buyer paid £16,000 for this top-notch MB. It was a very healthy profit.

Final test drive

The Willys Jeep was one of those projects that deserved a special send-off before heading to its new owner, so it was off to Upminster in Essex for Mike and Edd to take part in a military re-enactment. Kitted out in period military outfits, both the boys and the Jeep looked right at home amongst the tanks and other military vehicles, not to mention the odd Spitfire plane or two! The car

Those tatty seat covers had to go, so Mike sourced a set of original items from the States.

certainly went down well with the crowd, not to mention impressing an expert on WW2 Jeeps who was particularly pleased to note original features such as the fire extinguisher, the first aid kit and the identification plate on the chassis. It just went to show that all of the effort Mike and Edd had put in to getting the Jeep right in every detail had paid off handsomely. Nice job, guys.

I think the Jeep was the oldest car we'd had on the show up to that point, and to be honest I was bit daunted. There's a lot of heritage there so we couldn't afford to get it wrong, and it was another project where we both had to do plenty of research to make sure the final details were right. The toughest part was replacing the floor. There was a lot of work to do on it and it turned out to be harder than it looked, and involved a lot of lifting and turning of the body to get at it properly, especially for the welding.

It was well worth it though – I always approach our projects thinking of the future of the vehicle, and doing a job so that it will last as long as possible. I know Mike feels the same way and you've got to see yourself as guardians of these cars and restore them for future generations.

WILLYS MB JEEP 169

Wheeler Dealers – Series and Episodes

Series 1 – 2003

Porsche 924 – A dent was fixed at the rear, and body decals replaced. New parts included a replacement gear knob and stereo, and there was attention to the handbrake and exhaust, plus an engine service.

Saab 900 Turbo – There was a completely new interior, with grey leather replacing the beige cloth, while the exhaust system, brakes, and electric windows all received attention.

VW Golf GTI Mk1 – As well as refurbishing the 'Pirelli' alloy wheels, the gear linkage received attention and a new brake master cylinder was fitted. A new instrument panel finished things off.

Austin Mini – The rusty bodywork was sorted, the dented passenger door filled, and the car was re-sprayed in original green. A few new parts and an engine bay tidy-up completed the project.

Mercedes-Benz 230E – Work included replacement of the windscreen, a rusty front wing, and the steering box. A new fuse fixed the inoperative sunroof.

Ford Capri 1.6 Laser – Mechanical work included replacement of front suspension bushes, while the front wings were replaced and re-sprayed.

Series 2 – 2004

Toyota MR2 Mk1 – Bodywork attention included rust repairs to the rear wing, and plenty of parts were replaced including the windscreen, exhaust system, tyres, and locks.

Peugeot 205GTI 1.9 – A broken gear linkage was fixed; the cam belt and water pump were replaced; the rear suspension ride height was sorted; and new interior and exterior trim parts were fitted.

Suzuki SJ410 – With a new engine fitted, the suspension was modified and new wheels and tyres were fitted. The car was repainted in black, and a roll cage was added.

BMW 325i – Main jobs included fitting a replacement bonnet, clutch slave cylinder, exhaust system, and air filter. Various new parts inside and out smartened things up.

MGB GT – Rusty wheels were replaced and there was bodywork rust to tackle before a colour change from orange to red. Interior work saw the seats refurbished.

Beach Buggy – A rusty VW Beetle was transformed into a beach buggy with a new body and chassis, an upgraded engine, and a disc-brake conversion, plus lots of shiny new parts.

Series 3 – 2005

Volkswagen Transporter – A vinyl wrap transformed the exterior, the broken side door was fixed, and a new window installed. The interior received a bed and storage units, while lowered suspension finished things off.

Lancia Delta Integrale – Mechanical work included new suspension bushes, front brake discs, radiator and a replacement alternator. The paintwork was polished and new interior and exterior trim parts were fitted.

Mercedes-Benz 190E 2.3-16 – New exhausts parts were fitted, while the self-levelling rear suspension was replaced with a conventional set-up. New tyres and audio equipment completed the project.

Range Rover Vogue Series 1 – There was plenty of cosmetic work to do, including the fitting of a replacement rear door and tailgate, plus a new headlining. The transmission fluid was also replaced.

Mazda MX-5 – A complete new interior and hood were fitted, while major rust repairs were needed to the front screen pillars. A new air filter and suspension braces improved performance, and there were cosmetic upgrades too.

Porsche 928 – Bodywork repairs were a major part of the project before the car was re-sprayed in original brown. Also added were new brake calipers, wheels, and a headlight switch.

Series 4 – 2006

Porsche 911 2.7S Targa – A reconditioned gearbox and new clutch were fitted, while the Targa roof was refurbished and the American-spec bumpers replaced with European ones. The engine was serviced too.

Jeep CJ7 – Replacement interior parts included the seats, hood, and steering wheel, while the mechanicals benefited from new clutch cylinders, springs, and shock absorbers.

Alfa Romeo Spider Veloce – A rust hole in the floor was fixed, dents in the front end were removed before being re-sprayed, and new headlights were fitted.

BMW 635CSi – A leather interior was fitted to replace the cloth original, while there was work on the front and rear suspension. New components included the exhaust system and door seals, and the correct alloy wheels were fitted.

Chevrolet Corvette – Work included replacing the faulty digital instrument panel, fixing failed pop-up headlamps, re-gassing the air-conditioning, and replacing the exhaust system, plus some cosmetic work.

Lexus LS400 – Work was tackled on the front suspension and air-conditioning, along with an HID upgrade for the headlamps and replacement wheels. Exterior work included attention to the rear bumper.

Series 5 – 2008

Mercedes-Benz 280SL (R107) – A rusty front wing was fixed, and a new hood, headlamps, and alloy wheels were fitted. The SL got a new exhaust system, along with new front brake discs and calipers.

Lotus Esprit S3 – A new leather interior replaced the damaged original, while the engine was serviced, the leaking sunroof fixed, and new shock absorbers, exhaust manifold, and cam belt were fitted.

Fiat 500 – A new and uprated engine and gearbox were fitted, while the colour was changed from blue to white with the addition of special vinyl stripes.

Land Rover Series 3 – The biggest job was an LPG conversion, while the cosmetics were improved by adding a roll bar and new lights, and some black-painted exterior trim.

Citroen DS – Work on the complex hydraulic suspension included a new reservoir. The headlights were swapped for right-hand drive items, and the interior was improved with new seat covers.

Bentley Mulsanne Turbo – The biggest job was a colour change from the original blue to Storm Grey, while the front was updated with later headlights and grille mesh, and the tired leather seats were completely refurbished.

Series 6 – 2009

Triumph Spitfire 1500 – Work included a replacement differential and new rear shock absorbers, while under the bonnet the cylinder head got an unleaded conversion, with new valve seats and guides.

Porsche 944 Turbo – The track-day conversion included racing seats with four-point harnesses, upgrades to suspension and brakes, a roll cage, and a power boost. Some interior trim was removed to reduce weight.

Audi Quattro – The scuffed and damaged bumpers were repaired and re-painted, while the Quattro also received new rear wheel bearings and a new clutch-fluid reservoir. Refurbishing the tatty seats tidied up the interior.

Volkswagen Beetle – Apart from a complete re-spray in light blue, the Beetle needed welding to the luggage compartment floor, while the engine was replaced with a reconditioned unit.

Jaguar XJS – The interior got a new headlining and wood veneer for the centre console, while mechanical work included replacement of the transmission oil filter and a steering rack gaiter. The bonnet and grille also received attention.

Ferrari Dino 308 GT4 – Jobs on the bodywork included dent and damage repairs and a complete re-spray, while the exhaust manifold was also replaced.

Mini City 1000 – Aside from a new rear suspension arm and new seats, it was all about the exterior, with a complete wrap in carbon-fibre-effect vinyl and new alloy wheels.

TVR S2 – The seats were re-trimmed, while mechanical work included a thorough check of the electrics, a re-cored radiator, and replacement of the brake servo and track-rod ends.

Land Rover Discovery – A new power-steering box was fitted, and the Discovery was converted into an expedition vehicle with the addition of off-road protection, extra spotlights, a roof rack and ladder, and a snorkel.

BMW M3 Convertible – The BMW received a replacement interior, as well as work on the electrics, while a replacement gearbox was the big mechanical task for this project.

Series 7 – 2010

Jensen Interceptor Series 3 – There was a rusty floorpan to deal with and an interior refurbishment, while the Jensen also received a new steering rack and brake master cylinder.

Ford Sierra Sapphire Cosworth – The tatty front bumper was re-sprayed and original wheels fitted. The interior was replaced, while a new gearbox and clutch were fitted and the cylinder head was rebuilt.

Volkswagen Type 2 – New body parts included a replacement door and tailgate, and the interior was fitted with the seats from the Sierra Cosworth project. A rebuilt engine was fitted and the project was finished with a re-spray in special metallic orange.

BMW 840Ci – The damaged nosecone was repaired and repainted, and a replacement windscreen was fitted. The engine cooling fan and leaking transmission oil cooler were replaced, and the alloy wheels were refurbished.

Triumph Stag – After fitting an upgraded radiator and new cam cover gasket, the Stag had its chrome trim polished and there was work on the convertible hood and the differential.

Bond Bug 700ES – Plenty of new parts were fitted, including rear brake shoes and half-shaft oil seals, along with a replacement gearbox and lift-up canopy.

Volvo P1800 – With the carburettors rebuilt and the cylinder head converted for unleaded fuel, the Volvo got a replacement fuel tank and sender unit, front springs and shock absorbers, and fuel gauge.

Land Rover 90 – The Landie was transformed, with a colour change to metallic grey, an updated grille, new steering wheel and seat bases, new alloy wheels, and a replacement camshaft for extra power.

Subaru Impreza WRX – The biggest job was replacing the clutch, but the WRX also benefited from upgraded brakes and wheels. Performance was boosted by replacing the air filter and exhaust, and remapping the engine ECU.

Lotus Elan S3 – After a re-spray in red and white plenty of new parts were fitted, including an exhaust, suspension ball joints, and CV-jointed driveshafts to replace the rubber couplings.

Series 8 – 2011

Jaguar E-Type Series 3 – There was work on the bonnet air-scoop and the sills, and a complete new exhaust was fitted. A leaking differential oil seal was replaced and there was a light interior refurbishment.

Mini Moke – With an area of chassis rust fixed, the Moke got a cooling system upgrade, new coil-spring suspension, and a new hood and interior.

Range Rover P38 – A replacement air suspension pump and satellite navigation unit were fitted, but additional work included new anti-roll bar bushes and headlamps/front grille, a fix for the driver's electric window, and tinting film for the back windows.

Frogeye Sprite – After a colour change from red to blue, new wheels and seats covers completed the look. The chrome trim was professionally refurbished, and there was also a front disc-brake conversion.

Saab 9-3 Convertible – Engine work included a replacement turbocharger and ignition coil pack. Other parts fitted included bracing for the steering rack, a new ignition barrel, new gear knob, and electric aerial.

Dodge Charger – The headlamp covers were fixed, and the Charger got a new gear linkage and power steering pump, new front wheel bearings, the correct rear spring hangers, and a custom horn.

DeLorean DMC12 – With dents fixed and the louvred engine cover repaired, an engine oil seal was replaced, the interior was refurbished with new seat covers and carpets, and new electric window motors were fitted.

Chevrolet Stepside Pick-up – The loadbay floor was replaced with new wood, the cab received a soundproofing kit, the engine was upgraded with twin carburettors, and there was new chrome and new wheels.

VW Karmann Ghia Convertible – There was attention to the paintwork, and the engine was removed and the engine bay refurbished. The gearbox was fixed and the interior was refreshed with new parts.

Chevrolet Bel Air – The biggest job was a re-spray in yellow and white, and plenty of new chrome trim was fitted. The interior was refreshed, and a new carburettor and air filter were fitted.

Series 9 – 2012

Fiat Dino Coupe – There were repairs to the centre console and new black carpets were fitted. Dents and scratches were repaired, the distributor was rebuilt, and front suspension bushes were replaced.

Morgan Plus 4 – An entire new chassis was fitted, but there were also upgrades to the front and rear suspension, and new wooden floor panels were fitted.

BMW M5 (E39) – Externally, the bonnet was re-sprayed and updated headlights were fitted. The alternator was rebuilt, and new front strut mounts were fitted along with new mirrors and refurbished alloy wheels.

Alpine A310 – The headlamps were repaired and new rear wheel bearings fitted. A new water pump was fitted, along with a custom inlet manifold with new carburettor.

Porsche 914 – The engine was rebuilt with new injector seals, tinware, and a new oil cooler. Overheating was fixed, the targa roof panel refurbished, the wheels were polished, and the interior was cleaned and new seat covers fitted.

Mercedes-Benz G-Wagen – The front end was updated with a new grille and bumper, LED rear light units were fitted, the centre console was repaired, a rusty battery tray was sorted, and the interior was smartened up.

Jaguar XK8 – New suspension and brakes were fitted, along with new rear exhaust boxes. The throttle body was replaced, a new grille was fitted, and the TerraClean system was used to de-carbonise the relevant engine components.

Gardner Douglas Cobra – The rear axle was narrowed to allow deep-dish wheels to be fitted. The carburettor was re-jetted and a custom-made exhaust fitted to sort high exhaust emissions so the Cobra could pass the IVA test.

Jaguar Mk2 – Replacing the master and slave cylinders fixed the clutch, and the crankcase ventilation system was overhauled. The exhaust downpipe was repaired, while new seats and interior woodwork completed the project.

Willys MB Jeep – The gearbox was replaced while the damaged rear floor was replaced with a new panel, and the jerry-can holder re-mounted. New period parts were also added for authenticity.

Nissan Skyline R33 – The R33 got a larger intercooler, and suspension modifications and alignment for use as a drift car. Rust in a front suspension tower was repaired, and a strut brace and adjustable rear spoiler fitted.

Triumph TR6 – The cylinder head was converted for unleaded fuel, and the fuel pump was upgraded. A holed fuel tank was repaired, a new hood fitted, and the seats refurbished.

Isetta 300 – There were repairs to the rear brake and gear linkage. Rusty front wings were sorted, the body was repainted in red/white, and lots of new exterior and interior trim parts were added.

Ford Mustang Fastback – Front suspension arms and bushes were replaced, and the rear brakes and power steering damper overhauled. The front wings were replaced, the car re-sprayed in Highland Green, and the dashboard was upgraded.

Mercedes-Benz SLK – The faulty roof was fixed with a replacement hydraulic pump, bodywork rust was sorted, the wheels, headlamp, and radio were replaced with second-hand parts, and the supercharger and brake master cylinder were replaced.